DEAR PRINCE

DEAR PRINCE

The Unexpurgated Counsels
of N. Machiavelli
to Richard Milhous Nixon

TRANSLATED BY

Edward L. Greenfield
& Charles L. Mee, Jr.

American Heritage Press · New York

Acknowledgments

The translators would like to express their gratitude for the generous cooperation of one another and, among those others who may be named, for the considerable assistance of Harold D. Lasswell, Mrs. Ann Novotny and her research associates, Marcellus Winston, Adam Yarmolinsky, and David Rattray.

Published by American Heritage Press.
Published in Canada by Fitzhenry & Whiteside.

Library of Congress Catalog Card Number: 70–83813
SBN: 8281–0009–8
Book Design by Barbara Asch

Contents

∾

Dedication

NICCOLÒ MACHIAVELLI,
Citizen and Secretary of Florence,
to the Prince
RICHARD MILHOUS NIXON

T hose who court the favor of princes generally present them with whatever they possess that is most rare, curious, or valuable; as horses, armor, embroidered cloths, coats of ermine and vicuña, precious stones, etc., according to the dignity of the personage they seek to propitiate. For my part, my anxiety to present myself to the notice of Your Highness, with the best proof of my devotion, has not enabled me to discover, among all that I possess, anything that I esteem more, or account so valuable, as a knowledge of the actions of celebrated men; a knowledge acquired by a long experience of modern times, and a diligent perusal of the ancients.

The observations that I have made, with all the accuracy, reflection, and care of which I am capable, are contained in this small volume now addressed to you. And although I have not the vanity to deem it worthy of your acceptance, yet I am persuaded that your humanity will not refuse the offering.

It will, perhaps, appear presumptuous in me, a man of humble birth, to propose rules of conduct to those who govern; but as the painter when about to sketch a mountainous country situates himself in the plain, and in order to draw the scenery of a vale, ascends an eminence, even so, I conceive, that a person must be a prince to discover the true nature and character of a people, and one of the people to judge properly of a prince.

In your century, men have seen and wondered at the nurturing of vast companies and huge and haughty bureaucracies of the government, and greater and greater power has been seen to come into the hands of fewer and fewer men of trade, of the military, of government, and of sundry and divers institutions. Then, as it would seem, when your dominion assaulted and laid ruin your enemy in Japan by the use of the most horrible engine of war then known to man, the people did seem to feel betrayed by these few men and their remote and incomprehensible institutions. And thus did men withdraw into themselves.

As your government became ever larger, and your businesses too, and your other organizations and institutions, men labored to make of themselves their own individual duchies, disengaged from any order outside themselves, and assuaged their wounds by ever more and more acquisition of the goods of this world.

Then, as it would seem, your artists did cease to mourn the absurdity of the world and came out to your theaters and places of music to join together and celebrate their pleasures. Then, as your spoliation of Vietnam aroused them, they became more public men. And, no doubt, others would find a multitude of particulars to point to in the beginnings of this return to public life. Yet still, and bewilderingly, they did not esteem themselves as members of your guilds or of your political factions or of your corporations, but deemed themselves rather as citizens (akin to the ideals of your Thomas of Monticello) who transcended as individuals any petty organization or group.

Thus has the nature of power in your land changed, as citizens may no longer be manipulated through your traditional factions or groups but insist upon regarding themselves as citizens. And nothing could be of greater danger to a prince, for this upsurge of the populace is rare in the history of men and threatens to discommode or utterly undo the more ordinary political usages. Now, therefore, a prudent prince must learn to keep in balance all these individuals and give to them some sense of seeming or real power, lest they rend your dominion to splinters. For the duty that is yours, dear Prince, is to ensure that those things which you forge will provide for your own security and the endurance of your own republican faction in the White House for a quarter of a century. And thus have I deemed it well to speak herein of realities and not the wishes of those who would continue sentimentally to practice despised usages in your land.

I am not, Your Highness, insensible, in the world wherein I dwell at present, of the nature of the regard in which I am held in the world wherein you dwell at present. Thus, I should be judged a fool did I not cry out against my cruel fate, and beg your indulgence not to be dismissed by serious men as unscrupulous, scurrilous, maledict, discommendable, wanton, and suchlike. For I have been, and do remain, a republican, and my concern as yours is always first the preservation of the republic. And, as you are the Prince, and are dedicated to preserving the republic, it follows that it cannot be preserved nor can you preserve it, unless first you do assure your own position and hold it securely.

I thought it fitting to treat this subject as it really is in fact, rather than to amuse the imagination with visionary models of republics and governments that have never existed. For the manner in which men live is so different from the manner in which they ought to live, that he who deviates from the common course of practice, and endeavors to act as duty and virtue dictate, necessarily ensures his own ruin rather than his own preservation. Thus a man who wishes to be good in all respects and make of virtue a habit must necessarily come to grief among so many who are evilly disposed. A prince who wishes to maintain his power ought therefore to learn how not to be good, and to use that knowledge as circumstances and the exigencies of his own affairs may require.

If all men were virtuous, it cannot be confuted that one should be good in return, but because men are wretched creatures who will not keep their word to you, there is no need to keep your word to them. A prudent ruler cannot, and should not, honor his word when it places him at a disadvantage, and when the causes for which he first made a promise no longer endure.

But, as I wish not to be so terse as to be obscure, nor have I the desire to be prolix and embellish my work with long phrases or other meretricious ornaments or belabor my arguments so as to be obtuse or obfuscating once my argument has been presented. And I am confident, Your

Highness, that you have little need of such general, cautionary precepts and dicta as these. For neither am I ignorant of the reputation you hold in your world, and thus I am confident that by your character and experience you will sympathize with my work and be generous in your consideration where your greater knowledge makes mine appear wanting. I trust, therefore, that Your Highness will accept this little gift in the spirit in which it is offered, from,

your humble servant,

N. MACHIAVELLI

Ruminations upon Men and Their Times and How Different Times Are Like to Differ

As times are wont to change, so are the men who live in different times like to differ one from the other, for all men are the victims and the beneficiaries of history. It is manifest, therefore, that some goodly portion of my first edition of *The Prince* should seem to you specious, lacking in pertinence, or otherwise merely diverting. And this proceeds from two causes: first, that divers revolutions have occurred in the centuries that separate my times from your own and, secondly, that new philosophies have changed men's thoughts and the manner in which they speak and write.

As to revolutions, three things make your times different from mine, and those are the nature of the methods of producing goods and distributing them about the world and among peoples, the manner of your communicating in both time and space between men and provinces or regions of the world, and, finally, the very magnitude of things and multitude of people in your world. In my times, the citizens of Florence numbered some sixty thousand souls, and princes of my day were mindful of a world of only some several millions of souls.

In truth, your Prince Thomas of Monticello conceived a world more like my own than the one in which you now dwell. Yet since his time the novelties that have come into being have changed the very nature of your institutions and therefore of your notions of freedom, of the artisan's self-regard, and so forth. It would be well if Prince Thomas and the others of the fathers of your country could revise their writings as I do mine.

What would my world have done with your devices! Had the son of Lorenzo the Magnificent, namely, Piero de' Medici, who so brought his family into disrepute by his ill diplomacy with the French that he was driven from Florence and his house sacked by the mobs; had he had television he might have saved his reputation and fortune. For he, like yourself, had a dog, and this dog was named Bocci. And could Piero have come as a living image into the houses of his fellow citizens to appear before them surrounded by his family and speaking in fond terms of Bocci, he might have redeemed himself as you did yourself by speaking of your dog. For all men love dogs and love those who love dogs.

But enough of this. For it is unseemly of a man to begrudge another his advantages, and I do raise these matters only to observe that I am not ignorant of the manner in which certain novelties have altered the world since my days. Thus am I also aware that new philosophies have been expounded, and I have labored in consequence to read those philosophers who have had some part in shaping your times, such as the scholars Kant, Marx, and Freud (whom, I confess, I have not been able to read in great measure), as well as commentaries upon such men of action as Napoleon, Lincoln, the shrewd Lenin, and others.

Now, as my studies have been broad, yet have they also been at times too urgent or hurried or in some instances not profound. Thus it may be that you will detect upon occasion an ignorance of some new event or body of doctrine, or some inability to make use of the most modern locutions. For, as I know you must find my anachronisms (as my remarks upon fiefs, merchant-princes, and such-like) obtuse or amusing, so too have I found it not always possible to grasp each nicety of such neologisms, indeed novel concepts, as socialism, your CIA, etc., which are particular to your times. And for this awkwardness, I do beg your indulgence, knowing that you will understand such conundrums are unavoidable when men of differing times and cultures come to meet.

However, as my own times were found to be in many particulars similar to the most splendid days of Greece and Rome, and thus were we enabled to learn much from the ancient usages and wise men, so is your own dominion remarkably like Florence in its golden age—in its turmoil, its restlessness, its uncertainty in facing new things, and in its wondrous possibilities for achieving grandeur.

And while it is clear that my precepts have not been well regarded or comprehended by some effeminate men, as Prince Woodrow of Wilson, Sir Robert of Owen, the *condottiere* Trotsky, or the poet Eugene of McCarthy; others, I am pleased to observe, have taken some cognizance of my labors, as the baron Bismarck, the lord Talleyrand, the cardinal Richelieu, and even yourself, my dear Prince.

Therefore, and particularly in the knowledge that it will be sympathetically received by you, I am encouraged to revise my volume to make it even more helpful to you by adding to my own precepts some awareness of your differing times. And if I stumble over certain notions and rhetoric peculiar to them, I know that you will be forbearing and hear me nonetheless as a kindred diplomatist who speaks from the past to a world that is in certain aspects astonishingly like his own.

Of Foreign Nations
and the Balance of Power

I n 1454, Cosimo de' Medici, called Pater Patriae by his fellow Florentines, won the Peace of Lodi. And in that treaty, certain of the powers of Italy agreed to come to the defense of any other signatory to the treaty should that ally be attacked. And the enemy of one should be considered the enemy of all, and all and sundry of the allies agreed to maintain our beloved peninsula in a balance among the various powers to ensure the peace and liberty of all. Thus, as historians have ever after observed, was invented the notion of balance-of-power politics that has endured to your own day.

And as I believe there is much to be learned from ancient wisdom, particularly that which has been proved efficacious for several centuries, thus do I commend to you as a matter of course this principle. Thus also would I counsel you to continue your policies of keeping a balance of power between the Eastern and Western principalities of the world, guaranteeing always to keep for yourself some slight superiority in the balance.

As a consequence of this, two precepts are manifest. As nations, like nature, abhor a vacuum, so must you make certain that you leave no vacuums of power in those areas of the world in which a loss to your enemies would discommode the balance of power—likewise must you be ever at the ready to advantage yourself of any vacuum left by your enemies.

Now, in the maintaining of a balance of power, a prince

must have regard for those three elements which keep or disturb that balance. Those three elements are a prince's allies, his foes, and those others who can be accounted neither friends nor enemies. And in all this, these precepts are to be remembered above all—that the purpose of the Prince must be ever to make his allies stronger and better able to share his own burdens, to make his enemies weaker without so weakening them that they become desperate and intemperate in their actions, and to make of those not committed to his cause either friends or else render them incapable of becoming enemies.

Thus shall I proceed first to speak of your allies, as it is always well for a man to think first of his blessings that he can consider his miseries with greater fortitude.

෴

Concerning Principal Allies

Your best and strongest and most enduring allies are those nation-states that belong with you to the North Atlantic alliance and to its subsidiary military vehicle, called NATO. With these friends, then, must you make the cornerstone of your policy toward foreign nations. Nor must you ignore any possibility of strengthening them, nor must you abandon them. For, as all men saw, when Lorenzo the Magnificent departed from the ancient allies his grandfather Cosimo had won, and traded his good friend King Ferrante of Naples for the despicable Venetians, he helped to encourage the Pazzi Conspiracy, by which his brother was murdered, and to bring about a war against the Pope that almost cost Florence her own liberty.

Yet this alliance has already been in part abandoned or ignored. While in its military aspect it has been attended (albeit without consistent good effect) by you and your friends and has prevented your enemy Russians from unwanted meddlesomeness, knavery, or aggrandizement, nonetheless it has not been an archetype of cooperation and strength in other matters, nor has it been used as it might for establishing your power and influence in the remainder of the globe. And, in truth, it may be bettered in its purely military characteristics.

Your dominion has both great wealth and vast obligations. Yet because its obligations surpass its sources for wealth, it must be your policy to have your friends employ more of their monies for your common purposes. It is well to be liberal, but a prince soon learns that by being too liberal he loses the ability to be so, and thus must he learn to be liberal with the monies of others. It follows from this that your friends must not be your dependents or pensionaries but your partners. And this is a general precept that will be seen to be equally germane concerning your attitude toward those whom you account neither friends nor foes.

In your NATO alliance, you do possess ninety-five parts in one hundred of the devastating weaponry and of the burden for supporting those engines of war. And both of these must be shared with your friends. Thus will a prudent prince make fifteen partners of an alliance and not one great power with fourteen parasites.* And these partners will in concert determine when and whether your vastly potent weapons are to be employed. And your own

*Machiavelli apparently includes France among the fourteen. — *Trans.*

state, being the most powerful among all, would reserve unto itself only the unique privilege of veto. And all partners would disburse a more just proportion of gold to support this alliance. And while the Russians do voice fear of the German state having sway over such terrible engines of war and thus endeavor to dissuade you of this policy, the Russians are sly and disingenuous as you well know from your own experience. For their true fear, as is the fear of all nations, resides in that natural dread of seeing their enemies increase in strength.

You will observe that this policy will in some measure detract from your own independence, since your partners may dissuade you from yourself engaging in certain battles or wars or from the independent use of your most powerful weapons. And I should be accounted a buffoon or dupe did I suggest a prince limit his own powers without the most compelling cause. Yet there is some cause, and that is that a prudent man will always provide some device to limit his own fancy or his own passion if that fancy or passion, or the fancy or passion of his generals, could lead him to his own destruction. Thus may you be assured again that I counsel only that which will enhance your own power and prospect for survival.

Now this alliance must also be used, as it has been in some measure already, to enhance the trade of its members and to benefit their people, to make productive their farms and factories, to build great places of learning, to tend their physical well-being, and other suchlike things that increase the good of men's bodies and souls.

And, finally, this alliance must be used not only to the advantage of its members, but its members must in concert, sharing the burdens and the pleasures, use their might to enhance the trade, farms, factories, health, learning, and suchlike of all those other nation-states on the planet that it would be well to have as friends.

Here, therefore, as must be apparent to you, you have the design by which to build the most powerful political device ever known by man, with your own state, as the most potent among the partners, at its head. And as I am not insensible of the brutal manner in which my name has been so foully used by some of those generations that followed my own, for the sake of my reputation I would wish my name might be associated with something nobler than has often been the case. Therefore, if this modest proposal is of any use to you, I would beg that you might see that it is called Machiavellian. If it be too late for me to gain riches, it may at least be possible still for my name to have some luster.

Of Latin America

A wise prince will be neither dogmatic nor inflexible, neither obstinately principled nor too nicely moral. And I would not deem it necessary to repeat these precepts were it not that they have been most promiscuously ignored in your relations with Latin America.

These states in your hemisphere have been most lamentably flouted, even though it is evident that your self-interest is most mortally threatened in them, and you risk the making of a vacuum into which your enemies might rush.

Now, it is true that the Russian state has not succeeded

in having its manners and modes imitated there, nor is the insolent Prince Fidel of Castro greatly esteemed of many wise men in these lands. Yet you cannot rejoice in this, for neither are you well esteemed in Latin America, and you do tempt Fortune to treat you with an equal contempt there.

Thus, while the principle of inflexibility that distinguished your predecessors (excepting your Prince John) may be urged upon you to sustain a phylum or species of capitalism in Latin America, wise policy should dictate that that species be allowed to die out as unfit for these climes, and a form of socialism implanted in its place. And while certain truculent bankers and men of affairs or faint-hearted poltroons will shrink from this course and try to dissuade you of it, verity and not sentiment must ever be your guide. As you stand in a mighty need of partners, both puissant and small, as has been previously observed, and as you stand in a particular need to have men in your own hemisphere to be your friends and partners, and, further, as you may not win friends by standing by while they are made wretched, wise policy dictates this course.

Thus may three essential acts commence if not conclude the pursuit of your interests in Latin America. First, as the feudal manner in which lands are owned is the primary cause for misery in these lands, you must with your own gold or with the aid of others buy out the great and arrogant landowners and let them live in idle decadence in New York or Biarritz. And while this may gall some envious men in your own dominion, you may confound and rout them with speeches of justice or humanity or some such sentiment that can be found to cozen them into silence.

Secondly, your own oil and copper barons in Venezuela and Chile, who have of late given back to the people some greater share of their gains, must be imitated by all your merchants in all the lands of Latin America. And if this is not done, then with great suddenness your enemies will seize these lands and you will have lost all.

Finally, as the princes and patricians of these lands, by which appellation I signify the usurping *condottiere* and the great landholders, as these are all wicked and arrogant, they must be undone by means of new princes, new patricians. And to make new princes you must encourage those communalists who, though not your friends are nonetheless the foes of your enemies.

Now, these new princes will be heartened by the banishment of the feudal landowners. But, that more new patricians and future princes be found and elevated, you must establish certain schools to train a new peerage, as my fellow Florentines sent their own sons to the University of Pisa, or the English sent their sons and the sons of African chieftains to Eton, or as the baron Lenin professed the utility of "cadres." And to these places of learning you must bring young men from the countryside, numbering, let us say, some two hundred from each principality in each year, and they will be trained and taught to know the myriad skills and chicaneries needed to take possession of a state, and how to rule it, and then sent back to their own homes to win the love of their fellows and, in future, govern them. And, if some of these youths will one day oppose you or be lost to you, most will favor you. And, in any case, an entire cadre of this sort will cost but the merest part of the cost of one of your swift flying machines as have been seen to be lost in Vietnam.

From these policies that will bring you greater security

and more friends to share your burdens, we may also deduce this more general axiom: a cunning prince may always contradict his principles, as by the undoing of certain species of capitalism and the borrowing of certain expedients from his enemies and suchlike, insofar as it lies in his interest to do so. And he may always justify these actions with persuasive eloquence concerning themes such as justice and so forth.

Of Vietnam and Contingent Dominions

T here are those effeminate or hypocritical or otherwise myopic men who would counsel you to abandon the lands of Southeast Asia, and all on account of the disastrous and disgraceful course your former princes set upon in Vietnam. And this can be seen to be a mistaken policy from two arguments.

First, if you do not wish to have your unique attitude toward the Orient be one of mutual threat of utter spoliation by your most horrific engines of war, you must provide for the possibility of the use of more ordinary weapons, should the lamentable occasion arise in which you must do battle with the Chinese. And as these ordinary weapons are slow to be deployed and not rapid in movement or able to ravage vast territories at great distance, you have need of fortresses close to China. And thus any who would counsel withdrawal from these lands does in truth counsel a policy of mutual threat of utter spoliation. And while you may yourself not wish to do battle with the

Orient, nonetheless no man can know with certainty the intentions of another. And I have ever found it prudent to prepare against the worst intentions even while one wishes for the best.

Secondly, you cannot retreat from these lands because a prince in a republic is not omnipotent. And your Congress, with its several feelings of avarice or paternalism or morality, will not allow you to retreat. For they believe that your state has invested too much gold in this region of the planet, and that your commonwealth must not retreat until that investment has borne some fruit. And if lust for gold is not celebrated among the beatitudes, it is nonetheless a commonplace among men, and a reality to be reckoned with.

More generally, any prince must recall the lessons of history and understand that when Lorenzo abandoned his grandfather's policy of collective security, it was that act which led to chaos and war. And as your statesmen have labored in your own century to elaborate this same usage, it would be folly now to abandon it. Rather, the counsels regarding NATO can be seen to apply with equal force to your pathetic Southeast Asia Treaty Organization.

Now, as these axioms have been unaffirmative in nature, I shall not omit to mention what some would consider the most excellent aspect of your presence in these lands. And that is that if you will maintain a market place in this portion of the globe, you will see that you soon may trade with China. And since the days of Marco Polo, or even before when Palmyra lay at one terminus of the ancient Silk Road, men have dreamed of trade with China. For, even if its riches were not so magnificent as they were fabled, yet it remains a vast dominion whose potentates and people alike hunger for goods. And if one has prospect of trade with the Orient, it is ever a safeguard against depression.

Of Israel and the Arabs

As you must always seek to win new friends, so must you now let your wisest men consider how you may assist the Arabs and lend to their lives some greater dignity and comfort. However, a prudent prince will ask himself in this regard: How much did the Arabs upbear me in my recent campaign to gain ascendancy, and what number of Arabs did favor me with ballots in my land? For it is well to have generous intentions, but it is useless to have them if they lead a prince to an inability to effect them.

Whence it is to be noted, as you well know, that the Jews are one of the most puissant factions in your state and, if one can survive without their favor, one cannot endure if he has incurred their enmity.

Thus it can be seen that you must favor the Israeli state, from two aspects: that the disfavor of the Jews must not fall upon your head, and that you must not leave a vacuum in this region of the world for your enemies to fill.

It may be seen, however, that you may buttress the Israeli state without incurring the hatred of the Arabs too extremely; and this may be done by helping the dominions of Ethiopia, Turkey, and Iran to flourish. And these three dominions that surround the Arab states, as they increase in strength and comfort, will distract the eyes of the Arab potentates from Israel. Thus will you succeed in your policy in several aspects: you will prevent a vacuum from tempting your enemies; you will cause the Arabs to think that you do not discriminate against them purely for the sake of the Jews; you will not need to depend solely on Israel; and in all this you may seem to aid Israel, and aid it in truth, without provoking such inordinate attention to your policy.

Now, as you must favor Israel, it is to be noted that this policy is nonetheless fraught with vexation. For Israel is much like my own beloved Florence. The citizens there are frenetic and filled with anxiety. They cannot consider their station with notable perspective but rather live from moment to moment. They are, too, a very dangerous people, for they are angry and will fight alone if need be and will fight to the very death. And there is nothing more dangerous than a proud and angry and determined people, for they will think first of their dignity before their lives. Yet these tempestuous and meddlesome Israelis can be subdued, and very simply so, as your Thorstein of Veblen has shown. And that is by giving them the faith that they are secure. For, as Sir Thorstein has written, with security Israel will become like the Republic of the Swiss. And if all lands could be made like the Republic of the Swiss, a prince could well sleep at night.

Of Your Enemies

All princes live in fear of powerful enemies and dread the loss of liberty or life or riches to their foes. And as his enemies grow in strength, so does a prince's fear increase. Yet you do confront a conundrum both more reassuring and more intricately vexing. For you have two enemies, namely, Russia and China and their various friends or parasites. And neither of these lands is growing in strength in the same measure as your own might and economic well-being. This being true, you must grapple with the nice problem both of hindering your enemies and at the same time helping them lest, becoming too weak, compared with your own might, they become desperate and strike out in anger and frustration.

As I shall discourse upon China in the following counsel, I shall here consider Russia. For two decades this foe has not succeeded in winning imitators of its economic modes or political devices, in any land of the planet. (The unique exception to this being Cuba, though Cuba was less won by Russia than lost by your commonwealth through fear, stupidity, and, in general, appalling ineptitude.) Nor has the trade, commerce, and total sum of the fruits of their factories increased by as great a factor as your own, and this in a country that was, in the inception, sadly lagging behind your own. Nor have their attempts to improve their lot by various designs, plans, and devices borne fruit, but rather they have tried one course, then abandoned it, then returned to it, and so forth, and all to slight advantage.

Thus this enemy, while not increasing so in strength as

to embarrass you or cause you overweening fear, is nonetheless distraught or anxious.

And in this respect I never hesitate to cite the example of the Pazzi family in Florence, who, weaker than the Medici, became jealous of them. And, as it was apparent that the Pazzi had no hope of overcoming the Medici by forceful but fair competition, the Pazzi did grow desperate. Thus jealousy and the despair of equality or superiority did lead the Pazzi to violence. Had the Pazzi had some hope of becoming as rich and powerful as the Medici, they might not have resorted to violence. But the truth remains that they did despair and, abetted by certain friends of Pope Sixtus IV, they did attempt in bold rage to murder both Lorenzo and his brother Giuliano. And, as it happened, while Lorenzo escaped the assassins, his brother did not but was rather torn apart by no less than twenty-nine blows of the dagger. And thus can it be seen that a man or nation does not become less dangerous by becoming less strong in comparison to yourself but may become more dangerous.

From this it will be seen that your first concern must be to choose with utmost care those matters in which you frustrate the Russians. You may well anticipate that they will strike out again at their own subsizars or subject territories, as they did to Czechoslovakia. And you will know that such acts cannot be prevented or countered by your own forces.

Rather, instead of harassing or vexing the Russians, you must trade more vigorously with them, which would both enhance their own well-being and give them hope of even greater luxuries. And, as I am confident, this would be favored, too, by your own merchants.

Secondly, you must encourage visitations of unprecedented magnitude between your own populace and theirs, of at least ten millions of souls from each dominion to visit the other in every year. Now these visitations, and also such intercourse among your scholars, philosophers, and other men of learning will serve two purposes, and they are that your peoples will come to know one another and to learn to encounter one another more peacefully and also that you will thus have exchanged hostages. For there is a certain utility in the exchange of hostages to ensure peace, as your enemy would be less likely to assail your land if some tens of millions of their own people traveled in it at the time.

∾

Of China

I f Russia does not improve its destiny with alacrity or magnitude comparable to your own, China is even more downcast in this regard as it contemplates its future for the next quarter of a century. Its manner of home manufactures has failed utterly, its trade and commerce have little aspect of vigor, and, in sum, the Chinese cannot even fashion a method of feeding themselves. In justice, I must not omit to mention that the potentates of China have of late described in grandiloquent phrases and miraculous numbers their sudden improvement. But Orientals are known to be accomplished dissemblers and to proclaim what they hope will one day be true rather than to say what is the fact. And, even if upon this rare occasion they speak the truth, the reality remains that the numbers of their people increase, too, to gobble up their food as locusts.

Thus would I counsel once again that you engage in trade with the Chinese and thus, once they have somewhat to lose, they will be less venturesome and more docile—as they will not desire to lose what they have, nor will they despair and strike out in rage.

But now the most essential attribute of your attitude toward China is one that affects the Russians as well. For a prudent prince will recognize the government of the Chinese and beg to have them taken into the community of nations, and this for two reasons. First, because it is always well to be able to see your enemy and know what he does and what he may do, and if you close your eyes to your enemy, you err in the most basic manner that a prince may err and can be accounted nought but a fool or a madman. Secondly, by inviting the Chinese to join the community of nations, you will bring them into the arena in which they may harass and frustrate the Russians, thus both driving the Russians more to an accommodation to your own designs and discommoding those plans of theirs that cause you vexation.

In sum, then, your own attitude toward these foes will keep them content and hopeful while, at the same time, you will keep them from venting their frustrations upon your own state by setting the dogs one upon the other.

Of Former Colonies
and Backward Nations

In these wretched and impoverished dominions can be seen in your time all excesses and evidences of bestiality that were exhibited by the very worst of men in my times. These places, being of no use to you, are nonetheless a source of enduring nuisance and grief. For they are led by cowards, effeminates, or former savages who sleep in golden beds and keep costly courtesans. They are pernicious, vainglorious, arrogant, conniving, and ostentatious in all their ways, as the Prince Kwame of Nkrumah, who ordered a splendid chariot from the Rolls-Royce merchants for tens of thousands of dollars, and this while his own people remained diseased and impoverished and downcast. Not even Cesare Borgia was sufficiently audacious to have done such a thing. And they speak not the truth but dissemble and cheat and steal, as a certain Oriental minister who has some nine millions of dollars in secret deposits with your Bank of America, and I know not how much in Switzerland and elsewhere. And also pretentious, for in my times in Florence a diplomat customarily had but one morning dress, whereas in a certain dominion in West Africa the diplomats have three morning dresses as a matter of custom. And in the sty of Saudi Arabia, the sheiks do still keep slaves. And I have heard it said that a certain Indian minister is a contemplative man, but I know that when he seems so he is in truth only in a trance.

Yet these savages and Byzantine dissemblers must in

some fashion be accommodated or otherwise dealt with, for the conundrum of the races is the greatest vexation to be faced in your century.

Thus we proceed to the question of what these dominions love and desire, and the truth is that they love gold. And therefore must the Prince determine in what manner and to whom his gold is to be given. First, therefore, a prudent prince will give gold to those dominions that are significant to the security of his own land and of his allies. Secondly, will it be given to those who are possessed of some elements of value as timber, minerals, or other resources. Thirdly, wealth will be given to those lands that do provide new market places for the merchants of your own commonwealth. Fourthly, will it be given to those places that provide some manner of engagement for your youth, as your youth do need to venture forth and make new discoveries and feel themselves challenged as the explorers of my day felt themselves to be. And, finally, will it be given to those who wish to help themselves.

As I commended cadres to you to help to raise new and less corrupt future princes for Latin America, so do I commend that same design to you to be employed in Africa, India, the divers dominions of the Orient, and the other former colonies and backward nations. And thus it is to be hoped that future generations will know that dignity is the result of their own labors and learn to comport themselves as though they live in your century and not in mine.

Of the United Nations

This useless and dejected organization, which is held in contempt by men who have more regard for reality than sentiment, is purposely kept enfeebled by the great powers, who care not—as it contains no threat to their security—whether it lives or dies.

Yet this organization might be put to some use, as in helping the former colonies and backward nations to give more comfort to the lives of their peoples, and thus a prince might well consider how to make it strong.

Now, as all men are hopeless and despised unless they own something, so are all governments despised that are poor. Thus, if you would put the United Nations to some use, you must prevail upon all nations to grant it the ownership of all the oceans. And thus by lease or other device could this organization demand tribute from those that exploit its property, and put these riches to some use.

How a Prince Must Act in Order to Gain Reputation

Nothing causes a prince to be so much esteemed as great enterprises and extraordinary actions. We had in our own day Ferdinand, King of Aragon, and later King of Spain. He may be termed a new prince, because from the ruler of a petty state he advanced himself to be the first king in Christendom, and if you regard his actions you will find all very great and some of them splendid. At the beginning of his reign he assailed Granada, and that enterprise was the foundation of his state.

Thus, too, did your Prince John of Kennedy at once fall upon and assault the Cuban republic at the beginning of his reign in the hope of emulating the good example of Ferdinand. And, though his failure might have ended his reign, he courageously admitted the error of his ways and redeemed himself almost at once, as at once he had need to do, by confronting his enemies over the emplacement of certain artillery in that same state of Cuba.

Thus, too, did Lorenzo de' Medici at the first opportunity lay waste and despoil his subject town of Volterra, on the pretext of some minor disagreement over their alum mines, and inspire fear and astonishment at his action. Thus also, in the war that followed the Pazzi Conspiracy, did Lorenzo journey to the very midst of the enemy camp to win peace. And although it was not known to the Florentines, because Lorenzo had taken care to conceal the fact, he had had a prior agreement with his enemy King Ferrante of Naples and knew that his life was not in danger. Yet again did he inspire fear and terror, letting the Florentines believe Ferrante might murder him, so that when he returned from Naples with a treaty, they marveled not only that he had won them peace but that he had risked his own life in caring for the preservation of theirs.

So does history furnish many examples, as your Prince Dwight of Eisenhower had your citizens believe that it was he who won peace in Korea, risking his life, or so it seemed, by journeying to the field of battle; and so forth, as in Lebanon, and suchlike, and your Prince Lyndon of

Johnson in the Dominican Republic, et cetera.

Thus would it seem well for you to choose some small and weak state to assail at once, and no act gives a prince greater pleasure than to despoil some state in seeming rectitude and courage. Yet a prince must learn to deny himself certain pleasures or seek them in other ways, as time and circumstance alter. Thus would I commend to you the policy of more discreetly laying waste certain barons or potentates in your own land (of whom I am pleased to discourse in later counsels) while present reality dissuade you from following the example of your recent princes. And for a brief discourse on the new nature of war, I beg you to read the counsel that follows.

On the Nature of War

In my time, the generals of our armies had but one manner of doing battle, and that was to avoid at all cost engaging the opposing army in actual contest and to labor instead to do nought but lay siege to the cities of the enemy. Thus with large forces would the generals camp about a town and await the starvation or surrender or easy conquest of them.

In your own time, there have been three principal modes of waging war: these are the confrontation between vast and heavily armed contingents of troops, the reliance upon the threat of complete annihilation by devastating weaponry, and, as the Spanish so first referred to it, guerrilla warfare.

Your own commonwealth has relied upon the former two modes. And as those two modes have been matured, at the same time your world grew apart into two principal factions made up of those who resided in the Western Hemisphere and those in the Eastern. However, when it became manifest to both factions that the actual use of weapons of total annihilation was not feasible, your generals turned to the past and came to rely upon the older usages of warfare, while the generals of the East conceived —or as I should perhaps say, reconceived—guerrilla warfare. And now, as you have learned to your rue in Vietnam, it is requisite that your generals and other strategists invent new devices and manners of battle suited to the routing of guerrilla warriors.

As it is therefore necessary for you to have monies to create and manufacture these new devices, you must cease abruptly and entirely the making of your most potent engines of destruction.* For these devices that you have are sufficient in number to annihilate all men everywhere on the planet one hundred times. But, as a man may die but once, more of these weapons would be only so much more superfluous. And I myself cannot conceive that a man of reason would continue to be so profligate as to make more of these engines. And it is in any case the truth that these devices can be used but once, whereas a myriad of other devices and strategies may be applied with discretion in many instances and in proportion as the occasion demands. Thus, if your manufactures cease to make these huge engines, you will gain repute for a humane intent,

*I must not omit to mention in this, dear Prince, that your ABM, as one of your newest and most profligate extravagances is known, threatens to embarrass you potently —as it is such a transparent absurdity. And you would do well to discover some plausible pretext upon which to abandon it.—N.M.

while in truth you will achieve your aims in being able to afford new vehicles of war better suited for assailing your enemies.

Thus may I commend to you two new manners of war. And the first is the creation of small, brave, highly trained special forces, led by rugged *condottiere*. And let these small bands of troops be excellently well-equipped and have at their disposal vast stores of supplies kept by your friends about the globe. And let them be moved swiftly from place to place by your largest and most splendid vehicles, the newest of which as I understand are able to fly with wondrous speed to any place on earth. Therefore will you have greatly mobile and fierce bands of soldiers, as have been certain guerrillas.*

From this it may be asked in what manner you may come to occupy any land in which your enduring influence is necessary. To this I reply that in my day city-states were often occupied after their fall had been hastened by the spread of famine or plague.

And from this it follows that with the daring inventions of your alchemical laboratories you could make such draughts as would cause devastating effects upon a populace.

There will be those men of timid sentiment who will oppose this, but you may answer them saying that it is more humane to make a people gentle than it is to murder them. Your alchemists therefore may be charged to brew such potions as will make a populace sleep or laugh, or in general feel themselves docile, content, and of good cheer. And thus, should it be needful to you, may your armies occupy their lands for whatever term is necessary.

*It may be found to be advantageous to you in certain instances, notwithstanding my subsequent remarks, to contract with the special forces of Israel to do battle on your behalf at cost plus 10 per cent.—N.M.

I will not omit to mention that some draughts are unpleasant or needlessly devastating, as I am told there is a certain gas that the dominions of your day have agreed must not be used in war. And I am sure that there are others that would cause people to suffer without need, and all these must not be used. Thus would I say that a wise prince will invite all principalities to send their ambassadors to a conference which shall determine those potions that may not be used and those that may be used in war. And as you have agreed that this gas may not be used, there remains no reason that you may not also agree upon other such weapons that may or may not be used. And, indeed, your ambassadors may well confer on all acceptable engines of war; and it may be that in your advanced times it will be found that murder, depredation, rape, and so forth are no longer necessary to conquest, and that battles may be fought by less barbaric methods.

It now remains for us to speak not of war in general, but in particular of war between yourself and your most puissant enemies. For you and your greatest enemies may know that any war between you has in it too great danger, as any war between you carries with it the threat that it may acquire its own momentum and propel you to mutual annihilation. Thus it may be that the most powerful principalities will never initiate a contest and will also learn to tolerate those smaller battles that arise in remote parts of the world when they must be tolerated. Yet the devices for engaging in these smaller battles must be made convenient to you to discourage your enemies from wanton adventures and, when necessary, to engage them in a modest manner so that you need not rely upon only the most terrible engines of war. And as it may be that so many dominions will find battle too dangerous and terrifying, you must know that diplomacy, stealth, cunning, subterfuge, intrigue, chicanery, knavery, and suchlike stratagems may be the most often used engines for waging war in the circumstance of your world. And as I would hope that there are those in your realm who will understand such things as these, I shall proceed to another subject.

Whether Mercenaries or Citizen Armies Are Better for a Republic

I t is well known that in your land there are those who now advise you to disband your citizen armies and substitute for them a mercenary or, as it is called, volunteer army. And this argument is advanced with most ponderous historical reasoning, as that if a nation is to have an empire, whether by design or by default, it cannot depend upon the will of the people to maintain it. And in support of this argument it is said that the people will wish to do battle only to preserve their liberties, such as they did in your war against the Teutonic barbarians *et al.* not long since. But that they will not engage in distant border wars for less profound desires. And thus many imperial dominions, as Rome, Britain, France, and others, depended upon mercenary or volunteer armies to defend and aggrandize their imperial designs.

Yet there are three objections to be made contrary to this argument, and they are these. First, that history provides numberless lessons that mercenaries—as I have written upon many occasions—are inept, haughty, licentious, lazy, and withal do not fight as courageously as citizen armies.

The remaining two arguments arise from a single truth: that it is almost impossible to please the soldiery without discontenting the people. For the soldiery wish for war, and the people for the most part desire peace. The people sigh for a pacific prince, and the soldiers for one who delights in war—ambitious, cruel, and insolent, not certainly to themselves, but opposed to the people, as from such a one they might hope for double pay, and an opportunity of satiating their avarice and cruelty at the expense of their fellow subjects.

Whence it is to be noted that this natural division and competition between the people and the military is healthy for a republic. For the military keep the people from becoming docile and timid and despised, and the people keep the military from becoming too adventurous. For if the people will not indiscriminately support all ventures of the military, the military must choose its battles with care; and if the military choose its battles with care, it may with ease cozen the people to believe in the virtues of their desires.

A too large mercenary or professional army, however, as it does not demand the youth among its citizens to serve against their will, has no such natural check upon its ambitions, and therefore is it disposed to foment and engage in war without discrimination. This therefore shall be my second objection to a mercenary army.

My third objection does follow upon this: for, if a mercenary army will make it easier for the Prince to engage in war on his own desire, and without the necessity to win the people to his cause, it will also make it easier for the military to engage in war without his consent. And thus will a mercenary army, as always, become too insolent and powerful and tend always to usurp the powers of the Prince and bankrupt him by its constant and insatiable desires for battle.

Contrarily, I have never known of an instance in which a prince could not arrange matters so as to win the good will of both the people and the military when he himself wished to engage in a war. Thus is it seen that the temporary and inconsiderable convenience of having a docile populace is overweighed by the dangers inherent in a mercenary army. And the Prince will see that the advocates of such mercenary forces are only a few more, and those easily ignored, of those who envy his power and wish to diminish his office.

∾

Of Spies, Informers, and Assassins

Of all the sovereigns who best knew the manner in which to treat the poltroonery and the meddlesomeness of spies, King Ferrante of Naples knew better than any. For it was his custom to have them murdered and then embalmed and then kept in his palace attired in the habiliments that they were accustomed to wearing in their lifetimes.

Nonetheless, if this be a good policy for treating spies of the enemy, it is in most cases a pernicious policy if applied indiscriminately to one's own spies. Spies are evil, as history well proves; yet spying is necessary. Whence it is to be recommended that a prince extirpate his spies so far as possible while retaining his system of espionage. And to this end, I make the following proposal.

It cannot be confuted that spying is necessary, and in support of this postulate it is needful to adumbrate only a single instance of a matter in which it is clearly necessitous. And, if it were useful in no other matter, this one would suffice to justify the practice of espionage. For your intelligence agencies have what your astrologers and other wise men call a "model" of Russia. And thus, by giving into this model information concerning current events in that state—such as the movement of vehicles of transport, of peoples, and of material of various sorts, and this information being obtainable through the spying done by your artificial moons and other satellite bodies—your ministers can know very far in advance of the eventuality itself whether or not that state is planning an attack on your own nation by missiles and suchlike engines of war. Thus it is that it is impossible for the Russian state to launch a surprise assault upon your nation. And that protection alone is worth all of Caesar's legions. Of the necessity of espionage for the well-being and security of a state, *quod erat demonstrandum*.

Yet your own system is evil or otherwise hurtful and for the following causes: first, that it is a marvelous threat to the power of the Prince; secondly, that it is not possible to fix responsibility for its actions; thirdly, that for all its beneficent work, it is nonetheless too often in error; fourthly, that it is, in truth, for the most part useless; fifthly, that it is sesquicephalous and duplicative; and, finally, that its functions have been obviated by your wondrous technical devices.

First, then, I elaborate two instances in which it has threatened the prerogatives and power of the Prince, to greater or lesser extent.

In 1962, your Prince John of Kennedy only narrowly averted a grave and portentous international discord when one of his court attendants discovered altogether fortuitously that your CIA agents had corrupted a cargo of Cuban sugar with a nonpoisonous but inedible substance, and that this cargo was being taken by British vessel to Russia. Thus did the CIA take it upon itself to sabotage both the Cuban economy and the Cuban friendship with Russia.

It remains for us to consider the enterprise known to some in your government as Operation Camelot. And in this instance, it was a construct called ARPA, under the Department of Defense, that undertook to devise a mathematical replica of Latin America, for the purpose of anticipating rebellion in those principalities. And thus were agents dispatched during a time of political turmoil in 1965, and thus had the Department of Defense taken initiative in the conduct of foreign affairs. Yet, and humorously, was the operation confounded. For your Department of State—or, as it is called, The Department—discovered the plans of ARPA and revealed the Camelot disguise by informing the Communist press in Chile of the affair. And so did The Department do bloodless combat to preserve its own prerogatives. And, if you will permit me this frivolity in so grave a matter, it is also amusing to know that your Department of Defense, after recalling its agents there, and similar agents in other portions of the world, did nonetheless renew their contracts for researches —but that the contracts stipulated that the agents were to do their research in the Atheneum Library of Boston.

To proceed to our second and third criticisms, therefore, and to consider them jointly: that it is not possible to locate responsibility for the actions of your CIA and that its actions are too often wrong. Let it suffice so far as regards this subject to mention only the invasion of the Bay of Pigs in Cuba. And, since it is well known, it would be supererogatory to comment upon it, except to recall that your Prince John was a victim—whatever might be said of his intentions—of faulty analysis on the part of your CIA, and that it was so manifestly impossible for him to place blame on any agent of the CIA that he was obliged to take the unprecedented action for a prince of accepting the blame himself.

Now, as to our fourth point, that your CIA is useless. I quote only the opinion of several wise men who recently were disposed to make a private polling of many ambassadors, generals, and civilian members of your Department of Defense; and of these, 94 per cent declared that they have never obtained anything of value from the CIA.

As to its being duplicative, I need only remind you that both The Department and the Department of Defense have their own spies and informers, among those in Defense being Navy, Army, Air Force, Crypto, and others, all of which compete with the CIA. These being presumed necessary in spite of the fact that one billion and seven hundred fifty millions of dollars are publicly bestowed upon the CIA each year in addition to the discretionary funds of the Prince (one half billion) and the Secretary of Defense (two billion). What total sum is spent upon espionage cannot be known by one such as me in my private estate, as, indeed, perhaps it cannot be known by you. That the CIA is duplicative and costly, however, cannot be doubted. Nor can one imagine what secret enterprises are consuming these vast quantities of gold, although some of them are no doubt comparable to the project first advanced many years past of sending sausages and cigarettes to Russia by tying them to balloons. That project, as I am told, was not brought to fruition, though I confess it is a wonder to me why not.

Finally, the traditional functions of the spy are obviated by technical devices. Of this obvious point, that there is no longer a necessity for agents to lurk about in cloaks and ride at night in secret and wondrous vehicles or upon such common vehicles as trains, et cetera, little requires elaboration. There is a camera, as I am told, that can photograph a golf ball at the distance of one hundred miles and discern whether it is a Spalding Dot or whatever other brand. With duplication of effort, therefore, and with a myriad of such devices as these, your CIA suffers preeminently from an engorgement of information. Let no one therefore maintain that there is a necessity for your plethora of inept and despicable informers.

In conclusion, therefore, I urge you to extirpate entirely your CIA. Whatever information as is required can be levied in all matters political, economic, and social by The Department; in all matters military and paramilitary by the Department of Defense. This delimitation is to be strictly secured and preserved, and whensoever it is necessary for The Department to have military information, it is to request it of the Department of Defense and vice versa.

Finally, as to assassins, spoliators, garroters, cutthroats, incendiarists, terrorists, vandals, thieves, malfeasors, and other blackguards, let all their functions be performed by your Seals, UDT, Special Forces, and in particular by your Marines, and let these men be assiduously and resolutely isolated and segregated from the rest of your society. For such beasts are not fit to live among men.

And let all these informers, spies, assassins, and such-like be strenuously prevailed over by a committee of ten men, to whom both the Department of Defense and The Department report. Let them in turn report to a man whom you can trust above any in all your state. And that man you must watch as the fox doth watch the tiger.

Concerning the Divers Races of Mankind

I observe, dear Prince, that you confront in your times a problem both unique and unprecedented in the history of man, and that is in brief the division of the entire world into two opposing factions, those hostile factions founded upon the accident of color or race. And this great difficulty of the apposition of the races is bicephalous, for it concerns both your reputation and security among other dominions and within your own land.

Your foe in the Orient has well comprehended and exploited this unfortunate truth, nor will your foe cease to exploit it, but as he becomes more powerful it is upon this foundation that the Orient designs to undo your power and cast you down. Indeed, the princes and mandarins of China and its fiefs hope to beget a revolution over the entirety of the earth forged from this fact. Thus in time will your foe give greater and greater help to the former colonies and backward nations to engender a sense of brotherhood and purpose among the colored races. Thus, too, will your enemy Russia draw ever closer to you, as the venom of the colored peoples is aimed at all white men.

Now this course is made more complex by the truths of the history of your own land and its customary regard of the black race, that your potentates and lords owned slaves, and that, once freed, the blacks yet remained in a despised and downcast state. So do the blacks now rebel in your own land, so will they continue to strive for power in your state. And this will be nought but an embarrassment to you in the courts and palaces of the world.

As I will later treat of the blacks in your own state, I shall not here elaborate this peroration upon their condition, except in one general aspect. And that is this—that if the maintenance of peace be the difficulty of first importance to you, no other difficulty is of the second order of importance but that of the apposition of the races.

As you did not, in gaining your present eminence, win the love of the blacks in your own land but rather gained the votes of only one in ten of them, this must be of some concern. And, as I would in ordinary course advise that you might neglect those who bear you no love, yet you may never win the affection of the world, nor enjoy sway over vast portions of the globe, until first the world believes that justice has been given to the blacks in your land. Only then will that majority of the world, which is colored, find your words trustworthy. Thus in the counsels that here follow I shall endeavor to roughhew the aspects of that face that will make you seem just when you turn it to the East.

Concerning Blacks and Certain Others

I n your state it must be conceded that there is no necessity for the existence of, nor use for the survival of, certain people. And among these people we must designate many of the old, many of the young, most of the blacks, and all of those alienated from your ways. And while I here for special reasons speak of the blacks, much of what I shall say may be regarded as signifying equally the plight of others.

But, particularly among the blacks, who can view themselves as a group or faction apart from the rest of your society, this aspect of inutility is especially acute. For it is this truth that causes them to be troubled and that also confounds those among the white race who would wish to bestow upon the blacks some sense of dignity and hope. For it cannot be doubted that if a man or a race have no use in the nation or state in which he is found to exist, it must follow that that man or that race can have neither self-esteem nor hope nor happy expectation nor heart of grace or cheer. That such a race must realize it could do no better than to disappear or destroy or, indeed, deracinate itself, that such would be the highest service it could perform for the good of its society, to cease existence: such a race, then, can never be anticipated to be of value to itself or its nation. And thus may it wander from town to country, from mountain to valley, from field to field, and from hamlet back to city, with nought to nourish its soul but hate and with no light to guide its destiny but that which comes from the torches held in its hands.

In your state the blacks, and many of the young and the

very old, are not needed as other men once were for labor in your factories, nor for keeping your account books, nor to explore the heavens or settle the land. And if the old could be employed to educate future generations and pass on their wisdom—as was the custom in my country and in other lands—you ask no such service of them and particularly exclude the blacks from doing such service. They are not needed to populate your cities or to grow your grain, nor, as you have shown, are they needed to help elevate princes to offices of state.

That they could be used in some manner is not to be disputed. They could be used to carry your mails and deliver your documents and other correspondence with greater frequency than is now the custom; but what need is there of that? They could be used as wolves are used: to fight. They could be used as hogs are used: to consume your excesses of produce. But if they cannot be shown to be either needed or used as men, then can they never comport themselves as men.

Now, that this conundrum plagues others of your people cannot be negated: the old who are neither rich nor valued by their children; the young who have no love for your traditions and customary usages; the wretched and impoverished white men in your southern and mountainous provinces; and others. But many old are loved, and many young feel themselves to be valued by their elders, and the wretched whites can conceive themselves as members of a group that is needful in its kind to the state. Thus, although they are men without favors or riches, they do content themselves with hope and with the prospect or memory of dignity. And with efforts of their countrymen to relieve their fortunes, they are capable of becoming useful citizens. Were they black, and as easily isolated and esteemed by themselves and others as useless, they, too, should be cast down; and their futures, too, would offer no better prospects than the despair of their pasts.

Yet there is in history the example of a people who wandered from nation to nation in search of a home, and in your epoch they have been given their home, and I refer to the Jews. Thus would I make bold to say that a prudent prince will provide for the blacks their own home, their own city-states; and as it would be absurd folly to suggest the blacks return to Africa, I submit that they can find their homes in separate city-states within present white city-states and in newly settled towns and villages in your vacant lands as Utah, Wyoming, Nevada, and such-like.

You will not be ignorant of the fact that a group of your wise men conjoined to draw the designs for such new constructs at the direction of some of Prince Lyndon's court attendants. And their design envisioned only new subject nations within such present city-states as New York. Yet, in microc ism, their designs will suffice for our purposes. For they conceived of small contingent squares of a hectare more or less in which only blacks would dwell. And in these city-states the populace would both live and labor and, within the broad precepts set forth by the larger city-state of New York, would chart their own destinies as to new buildings, both factories and dwellings, tasks of labor, the nurture and education of their children, and all the other joys and sorrows attendant upon the making of one's own fortune.

I must not neglect to observe an essential aspect of this design, which is that in some ghettos in which blacks have lived, their greatest foe has been lack of gold. For it is well known that whatever fortune does result from their labors does in large measure leave their ghettos, taken by merchants and traders and other entrepreneurs to be spent in, and to enrich, other parts of your land. Thus it would be necessary for these black city-states to have, as all foreign countries do have, their own notes, bills of trade, and other currency that would in great degree and by law be restricted and not transferable to other currencies, thus ensuring its continued use and contingent growth in the black states. And I shall be bold to suggest that these notes and suchlike have the likenesses of black barons incised on them, such as their prophets Martin Luther King and Malcolm X.

But, as it is ever more advantageous to buy a new colt than to feed an old mare oats, so is it inevitable that you must build new states rather than try to revive old ruins. And so must your own monies—as state funds will be necessary at the first—be devoted *in primus* to the development of new states. And these states may be founded to advantage in such provinces as Utah and Wyoming and in other provinces that are becoming vacant, as Maine and Vermont.

Thus, dwelling in their own city-states, exalting their own princes and barons, and exulting in their own customs will these blacks become needful and necessary unto themselves and acquire dignity and self-esteem. And they will name barons to appear before your tribunals and walk with pride in your palaces of states. Nor will they ravage nor plunder nor burn.

Whence it is to be observed that we speak herein of the dignity of man, and I will be bold to say that the principal duty of the Prince, should he wish for glory and illustriousness, is precisely to give dignity to man. One may name history's proudest men and see that all have regarded this duty well, and those who sought power only for the sake of power have been esteemed despicable tyrants. If then a prince seeks not to be adjudged a brute by posterity, he will take counsel with the ancients and give his fellow men hope and dignity. Thus and thus only will the future treat him well.

Now, lest I be mistaken at my word, I must hasten to declare that there are some who would counsel you to make of this design for separate city-states a sort of ghetto as the Venetians had for the Jews, or a place set aside, as you had for your native Indians in America, where a race was forced to live against their wishes. And this I do not counsel. For this would serve only to increase the despair and lack of self-esteem among the blacks, or the young, or whomever you make these city-states to accommodate. What gives a man dignity is nothing more or less, as the ancients well knew, than the ability to exercise that quality which sets him apart from the animals, and that is his free will. That is, man to be man must have choice.

Thus, as America's blacks have never had a home and you will give them homes, they must be free to choose whether to dwell in these separate city-states, or to stay in your land, or to emigrate from their homes into your land. And, for those who choose to dwell in your land, they must be expected to participate both in the duties and fruits of your commonwealth. Thus must there be hope for them in having dwellings, education, tasks of labor, the rights of citizens, and suchlike. And, as various designs for dwelling, labor, and so forth have all been long since conceived, considered, refined, fructified, elaborated, enhanced, amended, mellowed, and fattened, it remains only for you to act upon them. I decline to sing the soporific monks' chant of these various designs; for the litany is well known to you and requires only a prince who will experiment.

And I am told that your commonwealth was at first settled in this manner—by men who were not needed in their European homelands but, given lands in the Western provinces of your continent, found need for themselves.

Though I may not deal here with your old men and women (who ought, in any case, primarily to be teaching your children), this usage may be seen to be efficacious for your blacks, and for many of your young and your poor white men. Therefore will you have done a good thing by bestowing dignity upon men and, as I am certain I need not elaborate, you will have taken the sting from the vaunted desires of some especially fierce and resolute blacks or have got rid of them. And though you will do a good thing, I see no reason to avoid doing good merely because it is good, especially as it is also advantageous to you. Indeed, you would be accounted both foolish and churlish if you forsook an advantage only because there was some virtue in it.

Regarding the Youth

Cosimo de' Medici admired above all other philosophers and wise men the Greek sage Plato. And although Cosimo did not heed him in all things, he did observe the counsel of Plato to "know thyself." And as I have Plato to defend me, I shall make bold to say: you must know that the youth of your principality have no love for you. And that would be a small matter if you did understand them, but you do not. And even that would be of no consequence, if the youth did fear you, but they do not.

Thus, as a lack of love and understanding and fear can lead to nought but disgust and indifference, it is no trifling matter. For as all men have known throughout history, the future reposes in the hands of their progeny. Nonetheless, if you can neither win their love nor their fear nor yourself understand them, how will they learn, and from whom, to make the destiny of your commonwealth their concern and alter presently their mien of insolence and indifference to one of forceful embracement of your land?

I make bold to suggest that the young might lead themselves with some little help from their elders. And to express the matter in a few words, I say that the laws of your land should be so altered as to have the students of your universities vote and select from among their number fifty representatives to your Congress, one from each of your provinces. These representatives might be as young as any student of your universities may be, but none older than twenty-five years, for at that age a man may take a customary seat among your members of Congress.

I conclude then by saying that as there is no hope that you can inspire their devotion, it would be wise to give to them the wherewithal to engage themselves in your government and thus find some hope and some manner of shaping their own destinies.

On Exile

I n former eras, as in those of the bold days of ancient Greece and Rome, those who offended the rulers, or transgressed the laws, dreaded above any punishment that of temporary exile or prolonged banishment. It is a measure of chastisement that has fallen into disfavor in your time. Yet it is an especially useful measure when it is directed against citizens who, having transgressed a statute, cannot even so be regarded as criminals. It is commendable in particular when levied against those citizens who, from sloth, timidity, or contrariness, merely decline to offer the wanted services to the state. To be brief, then, I would advise you to exile those young men who decline to serve in your armies. And as the places of exile for these young men, you might well ponder having enclaves for them in certain remote provinces, as in the poet Eugene of McCarthy's Minnesota and other regions in the north of your principality, near to Canada.

Of the Dwellings of the Poor

I t cannot be adjudged wise for a prince to promise his citizenry what he cannot give to them. Contrarily, it is well to promise as little as will content the populace and then to give more—for as the first course will cause him to be accounted niggardly and mean, the second will cause him to be thought generous and beneficent. I may adduce the instance of Piero di Lorenzo de' Medici who in 1494 promised the Florentines that King Charles VIII of France would not do them injury. And then, when the Florentines discovered Piero had given Charles a vast tribute to win his friendship, the citizens rose up and drove Piero in headlong flight from the city and were not satisfied until they had pillaged his palace, smashing what they could not plunder, and so reducing that haven of ancient arts and modern treasures to a ruins.

Thus, in 1968, did your Housing and Urban Development Act promise "a decent home and a suitable living environment for every American family," by building six million new dwelling places for the poor in the next ten years. That the promise cannot be kept is evident, nor can you be insensible of the fortune that will befall your cities should you continue to encourage such impossible expectations. In the past twenty years, dwellings for ten million of the moderately rich have been built, but only eight hundred thousand for the poor.

A myriad of innovations are required to fulfill even a portion of this promise, such as new zoning laws, changes in transportation, and so forth.

Nonetheless, these requirements are broadly discussed by many and are of greater technical sophistication than I have wish to burden you with herein. I restrict myself rather, as always, to more general precepts, and they are thus: that no dwellings can be constructed to accommodate your needs unless you resort to what are called previously fabricated structures for some large share of your requirements, and that nothing may be achieved solely by monies of the government.

Thus, to the essential precept, which is: you must lead

your investment banks and insurance companies, the very largest among them, to set forward equity money for construction, with a government guarantee, and that the amount of monies they must put forward amount to ten billions of dollars over a period of ten years. Thus will these private merchant-bankers ensure that factories and suchlike are clustered about their houses and other concerns are attended to. For only by the aid of their fortunes and attendance can you commence to fulfill the needs of your ill-housed populace.

And, while these same merchant-bankers may make vast sums today—what would be signified as usurious in my own times—in other enterprises, still this is essential. And you may inform them that the wisest of investors today are putting their funds into works of art and real estate, as it was in the golden age of the Renaissance in Florence. And, if you do not thus prevail with them, you may tell them of Lorenzo de' Medici, who descried that the international money markets and other merchant enterprises were unstable in the fifteenth century. And, when he discerned that the instability of the economy threatened his merchant and banking enterprises, he sought to retire somewhat from banking circles, and both by necessity and by choice, he did close his branches in Avignon and Lyons and London and other places and invest his funds in the lands surrounding Florence and in the city. And, had he foreseen the necessity sooner, he might have saved his fortune. But, like your own merchant-bankers in your times, he hesitated until it was too late, and thus did the greatest and richest banking empire of Renaissance Italy crash to bankruptcy shortly after his death. Let your lords of finance and commerce learn then from history—from the stories of the Bardi, the Peruzzi, the Medici, and many others—and teach them that their own fortunes and those of your state are as nothing unless their funds reside at least in some substantial measure in the security of the land, and their lives in the security of a contented populace.

And in sum I must not omit to mention that the day is passed when merchants from divers parts can impose their wills upon the peoples who live in your ghettos. And so must you make plain to them that they may profit as they can, but let the people guide their own destinies. For these men are only merchants and not princes.

Of *the* Rich *and the* Poor *and of* Commerce

A t the time Lorenzo the Magnificent held sway in Florence, that proud city-state was oftentimes embroiled in discords and battles, so that Lorenzo and his advisers, the Ten of War, found it requisite to maintain large numbers of soldiery. And to support these forces, the state had need to borrow sums of monies from the rich merchant-bankers at high rates of interest and to purchase from them divers materials to aid in the conduct of the war. In this manner were the rich merchants made richer, the while taxes were levied on the other classes in Florence so that the poor became poorer. And this policy had two pernicious effects, that the rich and poor became more disparate in Florence, and that merchants were raised to greater and greater power as they became more intimate with military affairs. Thus while Lorenzo lost somewhat the love of the people, he hazarded greater threat from the nobles he had raised to power, and his security was diminished.

Now, in your land is occurring a similar misfortune. For you have permitted to grow up great merchants commanding vast trusts; and these vast trusts and other companies increasingly have but one market place for their goods, and that is the offices of your Pentagon; and all the while, your people are taxed odiously.

Therefore, if you would safeguard your own security, you would cause these trusts to be diminished or divided. Secondly, you would work to lessen the resources of the Pentagon, whose monies in the amount of some eighty billions of dollars so fiercely prevent your entire economy from having some equilibrium and natural security in balance. Finally, you will seek to recover some thirty to forty billions that are not collected by your assessors. You must do this in fact and not merely create the appearance of doing so.* And this is necessary not in the name of justice, but solely because your manner of taxation works most perniciously against the health of your commerce; for many merchants now labor not for profit so much as to afford themselves some advantage of taxation. And as there are many philosophers who have justified a man seeking profit as the foundation for an entire design of commerce, there are none who have rationalized the founding of an economy on the basis of the search for some advantage in tithes or taxes.

*I observe in this that you have already spoken wisely on this matter, and I must compliment you on having thus stolen the march upon your opposing political faction.—N.M.

On Whether the Citizens
Should Be Disarmed or No

A new prince never disarms his subjects; on the contrary, if he finds them disarmed, he at once provides them with arms, for by arming them his subjects are thus converted into his soldiers entirely devoted to his service. The suspected become thenceforth attached to his cause, his friends continue firm in their attachment, and all his people become his partisans. But a prince who disarms his subjects forfeits their affection by the distrust that he betrays, and nothing is more like to excite their hatred. Thus it has always been a maxim that those who raise themselves to power, do arm their subjects. History is full of such examples.

However, time and circumstance change, and thus doth Fortune lay its traps for the imprudent. In your present circumstances, wherein the state holds the major portion of the armaments and has no need of calling upon the citizens to form temporary militia, there is no necessity for the citizenry to be armed. Indeed, their arms prove injurious to themselves. That they use their arms against one another may not be considered sufficient reason to disarm them, as I readily admit. Nonetheless, the Prince must anticipate all, and though it is a common fault of men not to reckon on a storm while the sun shines, it is evident that in your state the lives of princes are themselves threatened by an armed citizenry. Thus, and for that reason alone, a prudent prince will disarm his citizens.

How a Prince Ought to
Avoid Flatterers

I must not forget to mention one evil against which princes should ever be upon their guard, and which they cannot avoid except by the greatest prudence. And this is with regard to flatterers, as Arthur Junior of Schlesinger, who reign in every court. Men have so much self-love, and so good an opinion of themselves, that it is very difficult to avoid such contagion; and besides, in endeavoring to avoid it, a prince risks being despised.

For princes have no other way of expelling flatterers than by showing that the truth will not offend. Yet if everyone had the privilege of uttering his sentiments with impunity, what would become of the respect due to the majesty of the Prince? A prudent prince should take a middle course, and make choice of some discreet men in his state, to whom alone he may give the liberty of telling him the truth on such subjects as he shall inquire information from them—but on no other subjects may they be permitted to remark.

Thus may I cite as examples contrary to this good rubric Pope Sixtus IV, King Ferrante of Naples, and your Prince Lyndon, who neither heeded the wise counsels of the few nor ignored the capricious counsels of the many. For even your Prince Lyndon did not fear to silence or banish finally those voices in his court that privately spoke against him.

Or, in greater error, I may cite your recent Prince's reliance at first in rationalizing his policies upon polls of the views of the citizenry. Thus—it might have been predicted—becoming contemptible when, at last, he had to ignore such inventories as they came to contradict his own views. And thus he was made to appear neither responsive to the citizenry nor firm in his purpose, from which it followed, as plague doth famine, that he became little esteemed, his position insupportable, his office untenable.

A prince ought therefore to take the opinions of others in everything, but only at such times as it pleases himself, so that no one shall presume to give him advice when he does not request it. On the contrary, he ought to discourage attempts to advise him unless he asks it, and, upon any convenient occasion, cast doubt upon the reliability of the inconstant opinion of the mass, particularly as it is reflected in polls made in too many instances by ambitious men who care more for riches than for truth. By taking counsel with many, a prince who is not wise will never have united councils and will not be able to bring them to unanimity for himself.

Regarding the Exploration of the Heavens

I n your time man's ancient dream of reaching out to the planets and the stars has been achieved. And in this great triumph there are men among you whose names will be writ down with our great adventurers as da Gama, Diaz, Columbus—to name but a few.

And, although this last great voyage was begun by your enemy Russia, nonetheless when your people had that gauntlet flung down before them, your answer echoed around the world in the highest councils of state and in the streets and squares of the smallest villages. And without rancor or envy you took account of your own shortcomings and looked to know wherein your universities or lesser places of learning had failed, and you did improve them and did as well reply with your great riches and power and vitality such that you have now outdistanced your adversary tenfold, and have yourselves journeyed to the moon.

Yet, may I say, having accomplished this remarkable feat, having proved your own supremacy, and having awakened your own people to the virtue of learning in certain disciplines, is there wisdom in pursuing further this dream? For there are vast needs for your wealth in your cities now. And as all of the illustrious princes have known, the very word city is derived from that selfsame root word *civilis* that underlies civility and civilization. To sacrifice the needs of your cities to dreams of the heavens would be, therefore, at the same time both uncivil and ostentatious.

Now, should you declare as I think you must that your wealth formerly lavished upon the exploration of the heavens is now to be devoted to making your cities more vital, you will confront some bureaucrats of science or barons from such primitive provinces as Texas. Yet these men are old or weak and need not make you fear. But rather you must consider them as barbarians, as those who scattered the marble and gilded monuments of Rome, caring nought for civilization but thinking only of the thrills of the spoils. Nor, as I am sure, will you forget that *hubris* has never failed to bring ruin to a prince, though his destruction may take many forms.

Concerning an
Ever-increasing Population

I n many affairs affecting the way of the world, some of them being problems public in result but private in cause, a prince can do no better than set an example for his fellow men. Thus would I advise that you counsel your young Princess to have not more than one offspring.

On Law and Order
and Certain Barons
of Your City-States

A fter Cesare Borgia possessed himself of Romagna, he found it had been governed by a number of petty princes, more addicted to the spoliation than the government of their subjects, and whose political weakness rather served to create popular disturbances than to secure the blessings of peace. The country was infested with robbers, torn by factions, and a prey to all the horrors of civil commotions.

He found that to establish tranquillity, order, and obedience, a vigorous government was necessary. With these views, he appointed Ramiro d'Orco as governor, a cruel but active man, not unlike your own Attorney General, to whom he gave the greatest latitude of power. He very soon appeased the disturbances, united all parties, and acquired the renown of restoring the country to peace.

However, the duke soon found it no longer necessary to continue so rigorous and odious a system. For it was soon understood that the disturbances were the result not so much of the people as of the corrupt or otherwise bestial barons. He therefore erected in the midst of the province a court of civil judicature, with an upright magistrate to preside over it. He was aware that the severities of Ramiro had excited some hatred against him, and resolved therefore to clear himself from all reproach in the minds of the people, and to gain their affection by showing them that the cruelties which had been committed did not originate with him, but solely in the ferocious disposition of his minister. Taking advantage therefore of the discontents, he caused Ramiro to be massacred one morning in the market place, and his body exposed upon a gibbet with a cutlass near it stained with blood. The horror of this spectacle satisfied the resentment of the people, and petrified them at once with terror and astonishment.

Thus did Cesare Borgia deal with the discontent of both those who harassed and those who were harassed, and also establish a system of justice by certain reforms of the courts—which did him no harm.

Of Civil Unrest and the Laying Out of Cities and the Countryside

I n the fourteenth century and later, in my beloved town of Florence, the city fathers had cause to observe that the plan of their city conspired to render it dangerous to its very inhabitants in this manner: whereas previously men had built their homes with high walls surmounted by vast towers so that they could defend themselves against invaders by dropping stones and hot oil and suchlike on the heads of their enemies, these towers were now used by feuding families within the city and thus contributed to the dangers of civil strife. Little feuds became large ones, and small bands of rioters could wreak havoc among many innocent people.

Thus it was decided that the towers of Florence should be torn down, that the streets and alleyways should be made wider and more handsome, and that small areas of wood and grass should be set aside, both to keep the people from coming too closely and unharmoniously together, and to give the city some charm and pleasantness of aspect to maintain the populace in a more agreeable temper.

Now since that time, other city fathers have observed that their cities likewise contributed both to the ill temper and dangerous habits of their citizens, so that Vienna was designed to have two broad girdles of green land, and Paris was given its wide boulevards and pleasant prospects both to beguile its citizens and render it less difficult to maintain civil order in times of stress. And history is full of like examples.

Thus would I commend to you that your own cities be made more pleasant to content the people and better keep them in quietude. And for these purposes men have never found a better device than to make a profusion of woodlands and grasslands to keep their people from coming into too close propinquity and also to provide places in which the people may in sport and jest and game rid themselves of their angers and other humors that may endanger the state. These woodlands, in various sizes, may be placed both throughout your countryside and, in more modest size, within your cities. And a prince who is thoughtful of his security will know that he may never have too many of these places.

Secondly, a prince will make certain that his roads and city avenues are maintained in such order that his own armies and other forces may move upon them with alacrity. Thus in many cities princes have forbidden private men from having personal vehicles, as these vehicles only crowd the streets, befoul the air, impede the movement of goods and services, prevent the rapid movement of the Prince and his forces, and in general harass and annoy the populace.

Thirdly, a prince will make certain that his cities and countryside have fresh air and lovely waters that men may feel they live in health and vigor and have access to sports upon the waters and suchlike, so that not feeling annoyed in general they will not feel restless in general.

Finally, a prince will make certain that his buildings and cityscapes are handsomely designed, as pride in place, such as my fellow Florentines had, causes men to wish to preserve the beauty of their cities and not destroy them.

Thus, if your countrymen have lands that are filled with birds and other wild animals and places where they may find quietude and solace, and cities that are filled with splendid fountains and delightful grasslands and beautiful edifices, a prince will find that he has built defenses against bands of rioters that are as effective as fortresses, and that he will have lulled his people to a certain contentment as well. And a contented populace, surrounded by vast open spaces where armies may well form their battle lines, will be seen to be a people who pose no threat to their Prince.

Of Education,
the Trivium and Quadrivium

Elsewhere I have remarked that your institutions and practices of agriculture resemble those of feudalism, and I must make the same censorious observation of your institutions and practices of education. In this aspect: that they are designed not to educate all citizens in the arts of the humanities and nurture them to take their places as citizens in a republic, but that they are designed to maintain certain estates in your commonwealth, and within those estates, to raise your populace for no higher goal than to become skilled craftsmen and tradesmen and to produce and consume certain goods and services. Thus, in training your peoples to take up these functions, this process of producing, getting, and spending becomes the *modus vivendi* of your society, its common goal and its highest good. Yet the bestial making and consuming of things cannot be said to be the greatest activity to which man can aspire. Nor can the effort to make men content with this as their greatest achievement, as was attempted in the days of feudalism, be considered noble.

If a prince have regard for history and for the good opinion of posterity, he will engage somewhat in actions that do not merely preserve his power but also add to the glory and luster of his reputation. And no prince may gain greater reputation than by reviving divers values of the ancient world that all men call civilized and look upon as an age of gold. And if we attend such wise and glorious ancients as Plato, we shall discern that he prized above all else that society which ensured justice, freedom, and the cultivation of beauty, harmony, and the elevation of the soul.

And Plato, in his counsel for the ideal republic, did devote extreme energy and cogitation upon considering the proper forms of education for youth. For, if a polity is to endure and attain its lofty goals, then its youth must be educated in how to attain and preserve the values of the republic. And, for your models in this respect, you would do well to hear the voices of Plato, of such latter-day followers of Plato as Marsilio Ficino, Lorenzo the Magnificent, Pico, Politian, and others, such as your own Prince Thomas of Monticello.

Thus, if you wish to have a polity that prizes justice, freedom, and so forth, your young men in their schools must study and converse upon these subjects and not exclusively upon such subjects as account ledgers, geometry, the sciences, the conduct of trade and banking, and so forth. That is, to the old curriculum must be added, as was done in Florence in my day, the humanities: for, as your Prince Thomas said, in a republic the purpose of education is not to train craftsmen, but to teach the citizens when their freedom is threatened and how they may preserve it. And this applies not simply to those of your citizens who are privileged to attend your great scholars at your distinguished universities, but to all of your citizens. For, if a majority is to determine leaders and policies in your nation, it is more important for them than it is for the minority to know the proper behavior of a citizen. In the past you have excluded certain of your populace from the education of a citizen by saying that their intellectual capacities were insufficient to comprehend the complexities of the humanities and of politics. But as your scholars are no longer able to maintain that preference, your counselors now exclude them by saying that their background of culture and manner of upbringing preclude the possibility of having the understandings of free men. And so are these men still trained, and not educated, to take their places as peasants in a feudal-seeming society. But a prince, as I have said, must understand the truth, even though he may need to lie to others; and the truth, as must be apparent, is that these arguments are devised by men who dwell within the elite estate of your commonwealth and, by design or otherwise, prevent your state from becoming a republic. Of course, you may wish to attain glory by means other than the establishment of justice and freedom in your land; yet justice is a good thing and need not deprive a prince of power. And its nurture has ever won the prince who cultivates it a noble place in history.

Thus we may assume that your factories and merchants and bankers will undertake to educate men into the skills they require to be workers in your society—if not wholly, then in largest measure. And the role of the state will be to educate men to protect their freedom and perform the duties of citizens and have such a general education as will suit them in your world, which changes as rapidly as did mine, to confront each novelty or unusual event or process of the future with confidence and with an intellect that knows how logically to deal with any of Fortune's surprises.

With these broad precepts in mind, we may with ease judge of divers particulars which present themselves to you. As, for instance, mechanical devices: numberless wondrous mechanisms have been created in your day to teach children to read, write, speak, reason, etc. Yet if technical skills are of less import to the state than an understanding of the principles of political and humane reasoning, such devices may be seen not to enhance, and may indeed threaten, the education of your children. For a republic works among men meeting face to face and resolving their differences among themselves. Children not taught by men will not be suited to become citizens. Mechanisms, therefore, must be used in the most niggardly manner conceivable and then considered and reconsidered often to make certain that they do not subvert what the commonwealth wishes to achieve in educating its children.

Secondly, schools must not be governed by remote dukes and barons but by the families of the children who attend them and by the other citizens of their community. For the former course breeds, *ipso facto*, peasants and slaves. And only by the latter course may children observe and learn the responsibilities and duties of citizens. It is to be anticipated that this self-government will at first be tumultuous and dismaying. But citizens may not learn to be citizens excepting by being free, self-governing men; whereas to rely upon scholars and men of expertise to make all policies is only to perpetuate the ideals and realities of feudalism. The heirs of Greece and Rome have found this ever to be so; only the Orientals have been able to esteem mandarins for many years. Nor is the nurturing of citizens a policy to be despised only because it cannot be done with alacrity or ease.

If the Prince should wish to embark upon this venture, he must know that the voyage will be long and will cost vast sums of gold. Like a good captain, though he leave the handling of the sails and tiller to the crew, he will nonetheless firmly set the course and be certain that none of his crew deviate from it. He will insist that the ideals of the republic be treasured. And, he will not reward any mutinous sailors, but will give his gold generously to those who accept most readily the duties of citizens, knowing that others will follow these leaders. The Prince must espouse the goals, but leave to his citizens their fulfillment. And if the voyage be at first treacherous, and more difficult than it would be under a tyrant, nonetheless so were all the early voyages of my countrymen treacherous. And there are still new worlds to be found for those daring enough to seek them.

All other particulars, as what curricula are to be commended, etc., may be seen to resolve themselves if they are considered thus: do they lessen the man and make of him a tool of a certain order or otherwise lessen his pride and promise, or do they tend to make of him a citizen who may one day help to guide his land to those ideals that made all men admire Greece? Do they train him to take his place in trade, or do they train him to find his place and his glory in the commonwealth?

Concerning Peasants
and Their Farms and Fields

Many centuries ago in my country, there lived great noble barons who were possessed of awesome power and influence. And they lived in vast bastioned castles set upon the mountain peaks. And from their castles, like emperors, they ruled their vassals and their peasants and got from the fruits of their labors in the land some profits. And this hierarchy was known as feudalism.

Now, in your land, where divers laws and sundry institutions of state are most modern, in respect of your agriculture, you have progressed not to the advanced methods of my own time, but have nurtured an agricultural epistemology most clearly resembling the features of feudalism.

It is to be noted in increase of this parallelism that your agricultural customs resemble with equal clarity the regulations of your enemy Russia. It is, with the control of parity, ruled by your Baron of Agriculture and his fifty provincial sub-barons, through the vassals of the counties, and thus to the peasants. And the peasant is entitled to register approval or not of some two hundred divers declarations each year. And so your barons support some peasants who would starve and flee their farms if not supported by your state through parity payments.

And so your Department of Agriculture minions go out and, as certain researches have revealed, more than one hundred in a year serve, harass, or otherwise bully each and every peasant. This department presides over the Commodity Credit Corporation, the largest corporation known to man, and this corporation in turn influences more potently than any other man or men the prices, the kinds of grain and varieties of livestock nurtured, and thus, in sum, what both man and beast eat in your state. And this is no trifling affair, for more stones of hay than steel are produced in your dominion, so that these matters concern an industry worth three to five hundred billions of dollars. And your Department of Agriculture pays the peasants one-half of the net farm income in one year.

In 1933, the first conspiratorial faction of Communists was found inside your government, and it was found in this department. And these same *signori* who were said to be Communists had in that same year taken distinguished shares in writing and having the legislators ingratiated to the Agricultural Adjustment Act. And though your Supreme Court later disdained this law and caused it to be cast down as contrary to your Constitution, your farm customs and policies remain assumed upon that act. Thus, though locally elected, the members of this structure nonetheless take their commands from the baron above, and the peasants are powerless to be heard in their wishes. Thus is your system of feudalism, or feudal communalism, complete.

In Italy this structure of feudalism was naturally eroded and finally dissolved as capitalism was born in Italy and the Western world. And it may well be that your system could likewise naturally mature into capitalism, and have the structures of the state dissolve, and so turn Karl of Marx upon his ear.

This burgeoning of free entrepreneurship might be encouraged by the gradual withdrawal of parity price supports, forcing the peasants to compete with one another in open markets and thus driving some peasants off the land. In my times, the peasants came to the cities, where they found employ in guilds and various craft associations, but your cities need no more population to manufacture goods. Thus it would be well for you to encourage small industries in the countryside, as cabinetmaking and the forging of small tools, and employ some peasants as hunting wardens, keepers of the woods, and other occupations to which they are well suited by instinct and nurture. I note that there is some ease in this, too, as your department owns much forest and grazing land.

Then must you banish every powerful baron in your Department of Agriculture with great suddenness. And, finally, those peasants who remain on the land are to be encouraged, and your trade and commerce and industrial arts in general must be robust to support them. The solutions for the aggravations that will remain do not reveal themselves with clarity. There are those who tell you that one may break the glut of grain by persuading the Chosen People to eat pork. But I have not found Jews who are receptive to this notion. And if an excess of grain cannot be fed to hogs, it is as hard to feed it to Indians, for the gifts of your grain to India have served to weaken her economy and dissuade her own peasants from developing their lands. For this conundrum I have no ready response.

Yet it is manifest that your family farms are your most efficient and fertile of goods, as well as providing a bastion of liberty for the republic. The large incorporate farms in your dominion produce a small (three parts in one hundred) portion of your foodstuffs. The largest of these are the least efficient, as the Russian farms are. Thus, your family farms must be given the fruits of researches that only large farms and the state can afford, and so the state may help most by patronage of education and the dissemination of information concerning weather, markets, research, and so forth. So your families of peasants are to be encouraged to break their bonds and venture out from their feudal confines, and thus will you be able to call these men the heirs of Cincinnatus. And as my beloved Florence has been praised as a most expeditious midwife at the birth of capitalism, perhaps your own state can earn equal luster for having given to capitalism a rebirth.

Of Craftsmen and Their Guilds

I n your principality, as I am told, the craftsmen long ago formed guilds for the purpose of confounding those who wished to oppress them or cause them to labor for too little reward or under too odious circumstances. Now as to whether these guilds have aided the craftsmen or not, or whether the craftsmen have merely been afforded some advantage by the robustness of your trade and the benefices resulting from the policies of Prince Franklin of Roosevelt, I do not wish to contend. But these guilds nonetheless have become most arrogant. They are led for the major part by the vulgar, by former vassals whose fiefdoms are ruled by tyranny, who despise and keep in banishment and poverty your blacks, and who discommode your cities and assail your citizens and fill their lives with vexation.

Now as the craftsmen feel themselves ill used or badly rewarded for their work, as your blacks are not helped from their wretchedness, and as your citizens feel unjustly injured, you must for the security of your state somewhat assuage all their pains. And thus I commend the following.

First, the barons of your guilds must be brought to you, and you must, with the powers of your state to grant favors or deny them, cow these men and make them know what they are in truth, that is, subservient. Secondly, you must have them invite the blacks into their guilds and agree not to assail their masters with too frequent recourse to their tactic of concerted refusal to work. And, finally, you must give them to know that you recognize them for the vassals that they are and tell them that they may be treated as was Ramiro d'Orco if they learn not how to comport themselves as civilized men.

On Fomenting Enmities

It is by conquering difficulties that princes raise themselves to power, and Fortune cannot more successfully elevate a new prince than by raising enemies and confederacies against him, thus stimulating his genius, exercising his courage, and affording him an opportunity of climbing to the highest degree of power. Many persons are therefore of opinion that it is advantageous for a prince to have enemies, which by preventing him from indulging in a dangerous repose, will enable him to win the esteem and admiration not only of his faithful, but of his rebellious subjects. Thus a prince may well purposely foment some enmity so that by overcoming it he will augment his reputation and impress upon his subjects his power.

Thus did the Medici permit the vainglorious Luca Pitti to rise in their midst, to commence the building of the noblest palace in all Florence, and, indeed, for a time, to depose the Medici as the ruling family in that beloved city. Then, when Pitti ruled ineptly, he was himself deposed by the citizenry and the Medici returned to their place with even greater power and privilege thrust upon them by the Florentines, and the Pitti Palace left to stand for near upon a century, half-finished, no craftsman willing to set one stone upon another—a monument and reminder to any other who would aspire to unseat the Medici.

Thus, too, did you build your career upon raising the specter of a Communist menace to your countrymen in the province of California, and so, by conquering that awesome chimera, enhance your fame and glory.

The Prince must, however, take care not to raise opposition in quarters that contain genuine menace, lest indeed he fan some flames that will consume him. So for many decades did sundry leaders in Italy cow each other with the threat of calling the French down into the peninsula as allies against opposing city-states, until, at the last, the French were brought down to press their ancient claim to Naples and laid waste the whole of our countryside.

The enmity to be fomented must be one that is easily suppressed, as, for instance, princes may always oppose the excess of youth with impunity, since the unruly idealism of youth will in and of itself pass—as youth, like wine, will mellow by the natural process of aging. Yet, there are other enmities that may be fomented that not only increase your reputation but serve other purposes as well. In this matter, then, I commend to you the following.

Of *Civil* Principalities
and *Primary* Elections

L
et us now consider another point. A private individual may attain sovereignty in a civil principality either by favor of the people or the nobility. Whence it is to be noted that a prince who is raised by the favor of the nobles will find much difficulty supporting himself, because he is surrounded by men who, thinking themselves his equals, submit reluctantly to his authority. On the other hand, he who is raised to that dignity by the will of the people stands alone, and has few around him who would dare resist his measures.

From this it follows that there are certain nobles who must be cast down in your land, and these are the barons who come together at the great conventions of your political factions to nominate their favored personage for Prince. For these conventions, and the primary elections that precede them, are costly, insulting to your citizens, and foolish. Those men who are dispatched by vote to your conventions remain not responsive to the will of your people but rather still subject to the will of the barons. And while these barons hold sway at your conventions, the people are frustrated to see their desires ignored and, as a result, do come to regard all barons and princes and suchlike with contempt. And, in sum, when these childish and despicable conventions have come to an end, the man who would be Prince remains not the champion of the people but the beholden minion of the nobles, and those other pretenders to the throne whom the people may have loved most are shamefully cast down.

In this way do your conventions deprive you of the love of the people and make you beholden to many petty barons of your provinces. I say, therefore, that a wise prince will discredit and abolish these primary elections and put in their stead a primary election in which the people vote directly for the Prince of their choice, rather than for factors or electors of the parties. And in each party, whoever may have the greatest number of votes shall be that party's choice for Prince and shall carry the banner of his own faction against all other factions. Nor if this is done need you abolish your customs of conventions; for if they are forthrightly acknowledged to be circuses, the people will delight and rejoice in them, as the Romans well knew.

Let no one quote the old proverb against me, "that he who relies on the people builds on a sandy foundation." It may be true in the case of a single citizen opposed to powerful enemies, or oppressed by the magistrates, as happened to the Gracchi at Rome; but a prince who is not deficient in courage and is able to command—who, not dejected by ill fortune nor deficient in necessary preparations—need never repent of having laid the foundation of his security on his people's affection. But he who exalts his barons and wantonly bestows power upon them raises up those who may make him their pet or cast him down.

And should anyone reply that had these primary elections and old usages of conventions been abolished you would yourself, having been raised up by the barons, been vanquished, I would answer in the following manner. The tradition in your land is to maintain a prince in his station not for one but for two terms; and, to achieve this second term, the Prince depends upon the good will of the people and not of the mythical power of the barons. Thus, if you would have nought to lose by abolishing these usages, you would have much to gain. For by doing so you will have rid yourself of the unwanted barons and also would you seem to be more liberal and magnanimous, thus ensuring the love of the people. For circumstances do change, as I have said, and a prince must be prudent enough to alter his strategies to suit the times.

How a Prince Must Act and Speak

As elsewhere I have offered many precepts in a general fashion, I must nonetheless in several particular regards make bold to offer some especial axioms. First, a prince must never be seen to weep. Rather, upon those occasions when he feels the necessity to weep, he must do so in private or only among several of his intimates. And as you have some slight disposition to tears, you must be more aware of this precept than perhaps other men need be. For, as I have said, while a prince need not despise the love of his citizenry, fear is a more secure binding upon one's fellow men than love; and while tears inspire sympathy, they undo all feelings of fear. The report of tears seen in your eyes (in controlled and judicious dosages) by your closest counselors and friends at certain great and moving junctures may indeed do you some good; the same tears, if directly and publicly exposed to the gaze of the vulgar, could, to speak the truth, do you nothing but ill.

Secondly, if a prince must injure or insult another, he must make certain that his victim is so weakened that he will not have the power to revenge himself. And, though you well applied this precept against certain men, you most profoundly erred by insulting the men who write for the journals in your principality when you were defeated in 1960 and afterward. As it may be said that a prince never has such power as to vanquish all the journals in the land, it would be well to treat them all alike with respect, and make them all fear you by, upon one occasion or another, smiting this or that author upon some pretext and letting the others contemplate his example.

Finally, I have read your speeches and your writings, and I must tell you that I remember none of them. All the greatest princes have inspired their people and their followers with wondrous rhetoric, and it is their words for which they are remembered as much as for their acts. But if none can recall what you have said, how shall they know where to follow you, and how may historians account you nought but bland? Look to your rhetoric, dear Prince, if you have any thought of your station in history. It would be well were you to find some young poet in your land, and let him aid you with your rhetoric, and keep him constantly in your company. For this would accomplish two purposes: your speeches would improve, and that you were seen often with a young poet would enhance your reputation among the young in all the world, and astonish them, and cause them to respect you.

But, lest I seem caviling and mean of spirit, I may compliment you on many of your acts, and one among the many is particularly appealing, even though it may not be the most audacious. And that is in 1956, when your National Security Council was advised that the testing of your most potent weapons needed to be terminated, as no one knew what the contingent effects were in magnitude or quality of malevolence. Thus did you and your Prince Dwight determine to conclude your campaign for office with a promise to cease the testing of these engines of war. But your strategy was undone when this knowledge found its way to the baron Adlai of Stevenson, and he did remark upon this to the journals. And then did you distinguish yourself by naming the baron Adlai and Estes of Kefauver madmen and traitors or some such, and also, when the aides or minions of the baron Adlai attempted to steal the report on this matter that was in the archives of your Security Council, you made certain that the report was taken from those archives and destroyed. And I say to you, dear Prince, that it was an act that Cesare Borgia would have applauded.

Of Nations and the Seas

I would not, Your Highness, were it not a matter of such clear urgency and moment, presume to reprimand your countrymen concerning their ignorance of the seas. And yet, history speaks with such eloquence on this matter, and speaks such bold and forceful truth, that I cannot consent to be silent or I should be adjudged remiss.

In my day lived great explorers and adventurers, as Bartholomeu Dias, Christopher Columbus, Vasco da Gama, Amerigo Vespucci, and others, and they did embark upon voyages that did discover *twice* the world that had been known before them. And they were, and are, commended as venturesome and audacious men. Now, in your time, it is believed that adventure is well left in the hands of a few who in their aerial machines may explore the moon and stars, find new truths, bring power and glory to their states. I have discoursed upon these enterprises previously, and thus I do here abstain from comment, except to observe that if a man has his head always in the clouds, as it is said of Socrates, he is like to trip on the hem of his garment and fall upon his face.*

For as our Leonardo, too, did dream of flying, and our poets sang of Icarus, nonetheless, the wealth and power of nations was made upon the seas. From the power of navies and the rich goods that came upon the caravels, did Venice, Florence, Portugal, and all other great nations take their glorious names. And should anyone reply that the lands of the earth have been found and settled, and adventure is to be found in your time among the stars and not upon the seas, I would answer by saying that I am astonished that these critics see not that a great source of wealth lies still in the seas, and also new places for new colonies and great expansion of your state lie there too.

First, as to wealth, it is well known that the seas contain certain minerals and precious metals as manganese, cobalt, nickel, bromine, diamonds, and gold. And yet, excepting oil and gas, little or none of these riches are levied from the seas, and of aluminum and copper alone the seas would provide the elements for your manufactures for one million years.

As to food, as the ancients well knew, the seas are more productive than the lands, and yet man derives only one or two parts in one hundred of his foodstuffs from the oceans, and that in the most primitive manner. All this

*Here, of course, in his reference to Aristophanes' *The Clouds*, as in several other minor instances the reader will recognize, Machiavelli's recollection of the classics is not quite correct.—*Trans.*

while it is well known that some species can be transferred from crowded waters to others, as plaice was taken from Dutch waters to the North Sea and increased threefold in magnitude. And the sea can be fertilized by disturbing the bottom with jets to cause nutrients to rise. And men can be shepherds under the sea as well as on land and care for their flocks and establish farms.

Nor is it unknown that fresh water can be construed from the seas, as huge icebergs from the antarctic may be floated upon the currents of the sea, and brought to your parched province of California, and melt to many billions of gallons of fresh water.

And yet does your state spend only 250 millions of dollars upon the exploration of the seas. And yet you have been silent when an alchemist in Russia has said that a dam might be built in the Bering Strait, the cold arctic water pumped out, the warm waters of the Pacific pumped into this new-found reservoir, melting the ices, and making cordial the chill Russian winter. Here are riches, here the prospect of making a friend of an enemy by aiding him, here the hope of controlling the seas to make the ancient dreams of sweet gardens in hostile places come true. Here too, for a prince must not ignore his defenses, are facilities for secret and secure military fortifications, for safe laboratories, for hiding places for engines of war unseen by hostile eyes. Here too a place for new cities; here, Your Highness, is a realm for a new Poseidon.

And yet, I say again, your state has not deigned to spend on the seas so much as a pontiff in my age would spend on trifling vestments and baubles, or such as a Caesar would lavish upon a single banquet. If history will judge the naive and gullible man harshly, what will it judge a state that will not stir to pluck a grape, but will wait for another nation to seize the vineyard?

Here, then, is this realm, so sadly, so lamentably ignored since my days, that awaits its new Poseidon and Columbus. Thus I do not hesitate to urge your most sudden and resolute attention to this sphere. And for this purpose, as it must be that you have many affairs that beg for your eyes and ears, I make bold to suggest that you form a ministry or Department of the Seas or, as it is called in your time, of Oceanography, to have no less a place or distinction than you accord your ministries of Interior or Agriculture.

In What Way Princes Must Keep Faith

L egitimate grounds have never failed a prince who wished to show cause for breaking a promise. Men are so simple and so prepared to bow to immediate necessities that one who cozens will always find those who do allow themselves to be cozened.

One example, taken from the history of my own times, will suffice. Pope Alexander VI played during his whole life a game of deception; and notwithstanding his faithless conduct was well known, his artifices always proved successful. Oaths and protestations cost him nothing; never did a prince so often break his word or pay less regard to his engagements, and this because he so well fathomed this particular art of government.

Now a prince may deceive three factions, and whether the leaders of the factions be friends or enemies matters not for our purposes, for the same axioms will be seen to apply indiscriminately. First is the populace, and as the Prince makes such licentious use of promises before his accession, and of so many varieties both trifling and miraculous, numberless instances might be given of this. But let this example suffice so far as regards the cozening of the people: your Prince Lyndon, as is well known, never did anything but preach peace and good faith—as for instance he did oppose a baron who sought to be your Prince only several years ago by having your citizenry believe he was not a foreign adventurer but a peaceful man, and thus discredited and boldly injured his opponent—but he is really a great enemy to both virtues, and either of them, had he observed them, would have lost him reputation on many occasions. That his deceit caused him at last to be cast down and despised reflects not upon our principle of the efficacy of deceit but upon his ineptitude in deceiving, for he had not first sufficiently established an appearance of integrity. But, as this practice is well known and widely aggrandized, I will say no more but to remark if a ruler is to use deceit often, he must take care to appearances. For nothing is more necessary than to seem to be faithful and honest: men in general judge more by the eyes than by the hands, for everyone can see, but very few have to feel. Everyone sees what you appear to be, few feel what you are, and those few will not dare to oppose themselves to the many, who have the majesty of the state to defend them; and in the actions of men, and especially of princes, from which there is no appeal, the end justifies the means.

I say therefore in concluding that your Prince Lyndon was despised not for being a deceitful man, but for appearing to be one. For the mass of men, never being able to know what is, can and do only care for appearances and take offense at the appearance of evil, while remaining content to have evil practiced so long as they see it not.

Secondly, a prince may deceive the barons and lords of his own commonwealth and he may the more easily deceive them as they are themselves deceitful men and accustomed to being cozened without feeling the necessity of moral outrage. Thus again did your Prince Lyndon have rendered to him a virtual declaration of war against the principality of Vietnam by secretly sending armed vessels into the Gulf of Tonkin that they might be assaulted by his enemies and afford him cause fiercely to ravage them in return. Thus by stealth, and by properly measuring the poltroonery of his barons, did he achieve what he could not by direct measures. Nor could the barons and sundry other critics embarrass him by charging him with what he had done; for, by that time, if he had not the trust of the people, he could rely upon their timidity and confusion.

Nor will I omit to observe, as a minor matter, the manner in which Robert of Kennedy demonstrated how faith must be kept with one's political enemies. For it has been reported to me that upon the evening of the combat on television between his beloved brother, Prince John, and yourself, the baron Robert did cozen one of your own ministers. Thus, observing that you appeared pallorous and disheveled, with sunken cheeks and eyes, and invested in a robe and neckcloth that lent you an unmanly appearance, he could only at great pains conceal his pleasure. And when your minister asked his judgment of your appearance, he did reply, "I would not change a thing."

Thirdly, a prince may deceive his foreign allies and enemies, and one modern example will suffice for this.

Whence it is to be noted that your Prince Dwight of Eisenhower took great care to speak only of peace and disarmament, and to propose with careful scruple and noble sentiment his wish for brotherhood and harmony in the world. Yet did he with equal scruple appoint as his minister the baron Dulles, who threatened with massive retaliation and constantly gave his enemies to dread rapacity, plunder, sack, depredation, and sudden and awful spoliation by horrific engines of war. And so did your Prince Dwight manage often to speak nothing but deceitful words, and preserve his reputation of integrity, while all the time letting his enemies know his true intentions through the voice of his minister. And, had he been constrained at any time to soften his threats, either through the disgust of the citizenry or the genuine insolence of his enemies, he could have done so, in the manner of my own time, by ridding his court of his minister.

Of the Secretaries of Princes

A proper choice of ministers is of no small importance to a prince, for the first opinion that is formed of his capacity arises from the persons by whom he is surrounded. When they are men of ability, he is deemed a wise prince for having discovered their worth and found means to attach them to him. But when they prove otherwise, a mean opinion is entertained of his judgment from the unfit selection he has made.

Whence it is to be noted that Pope Sixtus IV was accorded contempt in his time for surrounding himself with his nitwitted nephews and ignorant bastard sons, and, as the princes of Italy could account him nought but a stupid man for having made these appointments, they at first preyed upon him and insulted and injured him until by force of arms he advanced his reputation.

But, as this is commonly known, and as it is of equal clarity that a prince may benefit of wise advice only if he surrounds himself with wise men, I pass to a less commonly observed truth. And that is that the sun is seen by men to shine so brightly in comparison with the other stars that are of lesser magnitude, and just so is a prince seen to be illustrious in comparison with the other men of his commonwealth. And your Prince Dwight of Eisenhower, understanding this well, took care to have as one of his ministers the baron Charles of Wilson, who by his indiscreet utterances made Prince Dwight's words seem all the more statesmanlike and considered and well-articulated.

Reviewing thus these lessons, I conclude, contrary to popular babble, that your choice of the baron Agnew is to be commended. For, while the risk was great in having him associated with you in your campaign, the rewards will now be manifest as his lack of merit and intellect make your qualities shine all the more brightly. And without doubt, the citizenry will cherish you all the more fervently and wish you well and protect your life.

I cannot in truth counsel you to pursue this course extremely, and I do observe that in your choice of Cabinet ministers, personal secretaries, and suchlike you have, perhaps, already reached that delicate boundary beyond which it would be imprudent to venture farther. Nonetheless, there remain some posts that could yet be filled by incompetent men, and thus I press upon you to consider the formation of a National Council on the Arts and Letters, to which you could appoint numberless effeminate, haughty, inefficacious, or otherwise unfit men, by whom you would be more illustrious in comparison.

And there are also numberless blacks who could serve on councils and committees and suchlike and, particularly if one were made your intimate and seen often in your presence, you would achieve another worthy goal as well. For by seeming to act with grace and generosity, you would seem not only illustrious but you would also split your black enemies, and some would fear your inconstancy and the others would love you; thus by dividing the blacks will you prevail over them.

Of Ministers of State, Sigmund of Freud, and Harold of Lasswell

Of the many novel conceptions and modes of perception that have been adumbrated in the interval between my own days and yours, among the most useful to a prince are those brought forth by Sigmund of Freud, Harold of Lasswell, and several other more minor thinkers. For, with an understanding of the significance of divers characteristics—as blinking, brow-knitting, the permanent creasing of the brow, the gnashing and grinding of the teeth, the sucking of the lips, the shaking of the head and shoulders, the throwing of pencils, the blushing in the visage, and so forth—a prince in your day may have an understanding of men far in advance of that which was comprehensible in my own times.* And thus are there certain habits or idiosyncrasies among your Cabinet or ministers of state that a prince would do well to understand for the purpose of efficacious use of these men. Further, as I shall in the succeeding counsel comment somewhat upon your own distinguishing characteristics, I shall here limit myself only to the most cursory and essential comment upon those characteristics, and only remark upon that most obvious distinction which in some measure dictates your choice of intimate associates.

To express the matter in a few words, I say that it is well known that you are a man of caution, circumspection, and calculation, and that you do fear spontaneity as a cat doth fear water. For, as the lord Harold of Lasswell would say, you do fear lest spontaneity cast you into an act either of destruction sudden and entire or into love complete and submissive. And as this proclivity toward either complete spoliation or complete submission is necessarily your primary concern, it remains to be seen how the affirmative aspects of it may be set free without setting free also the negative aspects.

Thus do we arrive at your need to create a certain surrounding or habitat that will permit you to release some impulses vicariously while others of them are given vent in

*I am not insensible of the fact that certain of your modern scholars have enumerated what they choose to consider my "obsessions": that virtue brings peace, peace brings idleness, idleness nurtures the beginnings of war; that it is wiser to be feared than loved, that nothing in this world remains constant but rather that all is in a manner of change, and so forth. And while your Sigmund of Freud and others might attribute these precepts to various aspects of my upbringing, I wish to assert that they are nonetheless true.—N.M.

fact. In consequence, I would advise you to surround yourself with ministers, in addition to your Cabinet, who are themselves spontaneous men, men of spirit, of quick rage, of easy anger, of soaring passion and conviction— yet men who are not so sincere in these habits that they furnish a threat either to you or to the republic, and that they also be reassuringly able. In brief, then, these men must not be so afraid of the truth or of themselves as you are yourself, nor must they be so vital as to cause you fright. And, in sum, it would be well were they vitally bland.

And, in the barons you have chosen to surround you in your Cabinet, I would make bold to say that you have thus chosen well, while I would offer the following caveats.

First, beware the man of flamboyant domesticity. Of any man who seems to have exorbitant interest in his family, and who presents himself to the people as a man who is in primo preoccupied with his home and family, a prudent prince will ask: As this is a shelter, what does this shelter conceal? And this may be seen to apply to several of your ministers.

Secondly, beware the man who embraces convention copiously, or ordinariness inordinately; for this man, too, may hide in seeming practices of conformity a frailty or overweening ambitiousness, as may be the truth respecting your David of Kennedy.

Thirdly, beware the man who is both extremely competitive and unusually shy, as is your Postmaster General. For as a man who engages in all manner of physical ordeal and loves speed and height and challenge may give you some vicarious pleasure, yet must you know too that great ambition is often masked by a certain guilty shyness, and while such a man may make vast demands upon himself, he will also make such demands upon his world.

Beware, too, the man who throws pencils, as does your Secretary of Commerce. For in such a man, rage or seeming rage is never far beneath the surface and may lead to impetuous acts, either of his own making or as he may encourage others to impetuosity.

Beware lawyers. For men who spend their days in court, as your Robert of Finch or William of Rogers, come to believe that problems may be resolved by definition and not by recourse to reality; they have a faith in the magic of words, as it were, and place their faith overly in solving difficulties by verbal formulae and eloquent invocation.

Beware as much as any the man who has made himself from nothing, as your Walter of Hickel, for he is ever ready to be made and made and made again.

Beware the blusher, for a man who blushes is a hidden lover or masochist, and judges deference to another as subservience to love, and may ever, if he is himself transgressed, work to avenge himself.

Now, above all, if you would well use your ministers, you must know how to cater to their peculiarities or else to modify them in some manner. And it is always well, therefore, to know these peculiarities well and study them and learn how to attach them to particular usages or targets rather than have them promiscuously contort or confound things in general.

Further, for those habits that cannot from time to time be made to serve a certain purpose, a prince must know how to pacify his ministers or keep them tired. And many men control themselves by sport, as games of chance, running, jumping, swimming, the riding of horses, the throwing of balls or javelins, and suchlike. And this is a meritorious manner of expending those energies that might otherwise overflow and confound their proper usages. And it is an especially useful way in which to dispose of these excesses if a man is a bad administrator and you wish to keep him from his position and out upon the fields of play. But for those of your ministers whom you would rather have in their offices, I may commend to you certain drugs or draughts or potions. And, as I understand that your physicians and apothecaries already have the habit of prescribing medicines, to the extent of one in three of the prescriptions are for these draughts in your land, to control or aggrandize certain emotions or proclivities of energy, it must not be too difficult a matter for you to place some of your members of the ministry on a well-considered habit of draughts, or purgatives.

Thus, in sum, may your ministers cry or shout or burst out in rage or laugh uproariously upon the proper occasion, and otherwise maintain their silence; and thus will you have surrounded yourself by seemingly incautious men, who in their spontaneity are nonetheless controlled, and have the vicarious pleasures that you must, as well you know, deny yourself.

Of the Character of the Prince

I n conclusion, dear Prince, I must not omit to offer you some observations as they occur to me from a perusal of Sigmund of Freud, Harold of Lasswell, and others who have treated of the psychopathology of men and of princes. Nor in modesty must I say that insights of this nature are foreign to me; for while they are of greater elaboration and sophistication, nonetheless I have been known in some small and select circles as a dramatist, and one who knows somewhat of the nature of men.

Thus, were I to portray your character on the stage, I should emphasize divers particulars of your character, as your inhibition, your caution and calculation, as I have mentioned previously, your proclivity to live vicariously, your choice of titillating ministers of state and friends, your fear of being spontaneous, the effeminate manner in which you shake your head and wriggle your body, the permanent anxious creases in your brow.

Nor would I censure these attributes. For a man is what he is, and if he may not laugh uproariously or give vent to easy camaraderie, yet he may have his beneficent qualities. And I should be the last to counsel that a man should change his manner of expression. For, as it will cause him unease or discomfort, so will it cause his followers distress. By seeing their Prince change, thus will they doubt their original perceptions of him and finally come to believe that none of their understandings of him are correct. Thus, if a man be criticized for seeming cautious, let him remain so consistently nonetheless, for he will then at the least give his people some sense of security.

Yet, as I am told, you have had the benefit of the counsels of the followers of Freud and such other men, and so you are not ignorant of your own proclivities but rather have learned well how to wear the mask and know that it must be worn. Then you must know too that a man who so rigidly controls himself must make some payment, and that that payment may be the sudden bursting out or gratuitous explosion at the most unseemly moment. Indeed, you will know that a man of your character may be illustrious in all minor crises but dangerous in the crises of true moment.

Therefore may I make bold to suggest that you provide for yourself, in addition to the titillation your ministers of state may provide you, some other people or things to which you can turn when it is needful for you to burst out, and for the rest some regular, ritualized pattern to keep yourself in harness.

Now, as it is needful that when you vent your spleen you do so with some feeling yourself that it is spontaneous, I would suggest that you preordain some number of targets to assail. Thus, when the need arises you may choose among these targets spontaneously. And for this purpose you may choose some of the states or potentates I have previously named to you, certain angry blacks, divers of your local party barons, the masochists and suchlike among your own ministers, and some barons of the Democratic party, or select members among your writers for journals. And in all this you must take care to attack not in a general way, but in particular so as not to bring yourself calamity in great measure but to have the pleasure of quickly and virtuously vanquishing a foe.

Finally, then, as to rituals that will delay or otherwise contain anger or impetuosity, the princes of my day found no better habit than the frequent and regular attendance at theater, concerts, readings of poetry and recitals, and other such refined and circumscribed events. Thus, if you may express your passion in music, or delay an act by the necessity of a private audience or public performance, and all this coupled with a certain ritual meeting of your ministers at set times during the day, you will provide a natural and illustrious barrier to vulgarity and sudden rage. You will, too, win a reputation in your state as a man of taste and cultivation and, thus, while you avert the beast in all men's natures, you will seem to be cultivating that which is most civilized. And it is this masterful orchestration of a man's own qualities that is, in sum, the challenge and the duty of the Prince. And, when he is successful in so orchestrating the finest and least commendable atrocities of his nature, his name will be destined to take its place among the most glorious princes of all history.